WOMAN AND FITNESS

Female body recomposition: workout and diet

©2021 Andrea Raimondi
www.fitnessedintorni.it

AREdit.com
All rights reserved
Contacts: info@aredit.com

=== Andrea Raimondi ===

©2021 Andrea Raimondi
info@fitnessedintorni.it

AREdit.com
info@aredit.com

All rights reserved. No part of this book may be reproduced by any mechanical, photographic, or electronic process, or in the form of a phonographic recording; nor may it be stored in a retrieval system, transmitted, or otherwise copied for public or private use—other than for "fair use" as brief quotations embodied in articles and reviews—without prior written permission of the publisher.

=== Woman and Fitness ===

Dedicated to Silvia.

=== Andrea Raimondi ===

=== Woman and Fitness ===

INDEX

Introduction 7
Differences Woman / Man 11
Female Biotypes 14
Water Retention 16
Cellulite 20
Body Fat 22
Energy systems 33
Kilocalorie 41
Energy Balance 43
Food Categories 47
Macronutrients 51
Micronutrients 57
Supplements 59
Lean Mass 63
Muscle Physiology 67
Mechanisms of Hypertrophy 70
Mechanical Tension 72
Metabolic Stress 73
Muscle Damage 74
Training Variables 75
Volume 77
Frequency 79
Intensity 81
Type Of Exercises 83
Progression 85
TUT 86
Rest Between Sets 88
Training Techniques 89

Periodization 97
Major Muscle Groups 103
PART II Practice 121
Dieting 125
Food Diary 125
Why We Eat Too Much? 128
Meal Plan 130
Meal Plan In Practice 135
Esempi di diete 138
Training Exercises 153
Aerobic Activity 195
Training Protocol 199
Adaptation Phase 200
Strenght Phase 210
Recovery Phase 219
Hypertrophy Phase 224
Strenght Phase #2 228
Hypertrophy Phase #2 247
Leg Metabolism Activation 260
Lunch Break Training 261
Lockdown 263
Functional Evaluation 266
Measurements and Indices 268
Motivation 280
Body Recomposition 286
Short Term Body Recomposition 292
Long-term body recomposition 302
Bibliography 307

=== Woman and Fitness ===

Introduction

The physical and biochemical structure of the woman certainly presents differences from that of the man. These differences must be taken into account in creating training plans and eating plans, but they are not so marked that you have to review the theory and practice of a scientific method that aims at body re-composition. The process that leads to the reduction of fat mass and the increase of lean mass is the same in both sexes.

If you want to lose weight, that is, to consume the accumulated fat, we have only two ways: to introduce fewer calories with the diet, eat less than you are used to, or to consume more calories with physical activity, with the same calories introduced. If you combine the two elements, diet, and physical activity, the process is faster and leads to better body composition and to maintain the results obtained over time. The same is true if you want to improve your muscle mass: you have to combine the right caloric intake and the correct training.

The contradiction, in terms of fitness, of the current opulent society, characterized by the great availability of food and the increase in free time, lies in the fact that it proposes as an example of a desirable body the lean and muscular body of models, while on the other keep people standstill in front of a screen, large or small.

The point is that you don't move your body enough: you just need to walk for half an hour a day to improve your fitness.

A better, more toned physique, with less fat, is within everyone's ability. There are few "rules" to know: the theory is simple. The

=== Woman and Fitness ===

problem is to put it into practice. With the exercises proposed in the book and the training plan described, which serves as the basis for creating your plan, you try to reach the goal for which "fitness" stably enters your life, becomes a habit. Knowing how the human body works help not to be dazzled by the bright mirrors of the fitness and supplement industry and the food industry. There are no miracle diets, there are no diet pills. There is the will that allows achieving the established objectives, through a path built over time.

In the book we highlight the differences between women and men, we will see the fundamental theory for the increase of lean mass and therefore the training theory and its variables, we will also see the food theory, the energy systems of the human body, the role of the various macronutrients. And we will apply the theory to both training and nutrition, using the role of some measurements and some fundamental indices to understand the starting point and the direction of the path. We will conclude with an example of body recomposition for weight loss and an increase in muscle mass.

In this book, you will find everything you need to understand how to build a training plan and a food plan. You can write to me at info@fitnessedintorni.it to join a personalized body recomposition program for you at a discounted price.

=== Andrea Raimondi ===

Differences Woman / Man

=== Woman and Fitness ===

Differences Woman / Man

In this chapter, we describe the main differences between women and men, intending to determine whether they are such as to cause significant changes in the diet and training approach.

Let's start with the **amount of body fat**. In general, a woman has a higher percentage of body fat than a man. The amount of **essential fat**, that is essential for living, is on average 10-13% of body weight for women, while for men it is 2-5% of body weight. Below is a summary table:

	WOMEN	MEN
Essential Fat	10-13%	2-5%
Athletes	14-20%	6-13%
Fitness	21-24%	14-17%
Average	25-31%	18-24%
Obese	>32%	>25%

In nature, nothing happens by chance, the presence of double the amount of visceral fat is the result of the evolution of the human-animal. In this case, the fundamental reason is to be found in the woman's ability to reproduce the human species. During pregnancy and breastfeeding, fat reserves are essential to ensure greater chances of surviving mother and child. The distribution of fat is also different, on average, between women and men.

=== Woman and Fitness ===

This distribution derives from the different hormonal profiles: from the presence of higher levels of estrogen and is accumulated on average in the area of the thighs and buttocks.

The bone structure also has differences that are a result of the evolution of our species: the bones of the pelvis develop in width, while those of man develop in height. Also in this case this conformation is evident to guarantee the survival of the species.

On average, a woman has less muscle mass than a man, therefore fewer muscle cells, myofibrils, and mitochondria. In general, less muscle power than in men.

The different role in the reproductive phase has led women to have a different hormonal profile from men (and vice versa), with higher levels of estrogen and lower testosterone.

In the table the differences between women and men in estrogen and testosterone.

	WOMEN	MEN
Estrogen pg/ml	30-120	15-60
Testosterone ng/dl	15-70	280-1100

Estrogen, as we said, among other things regulates the distribution of body fat, favoring its deposit in the hips, buttocks, thighs, and abdomen below the navel. In the female body, about two-thirds of estrogen production occurs in adipose tissue thanks to an enzyme that converts the androgens produced by the adrenal glands into estrogen. Their role is of primary importance in all phases of the menstrual cycle with production and absorption of progesterone, estradiol, FSH, LH, and all the changes that this entails at the ovarian and uterine level and in body temperature. In any case, I want to assure all women that there is currently no research that leads to a correlation between the different phases of the menstrual cycle and greater or lesser training capacity. For the record, I report that someone hypothesizes instead a greater increase in strength and the relative amount of training to undergo during the follicular phase of the menstrual cycle (before menstruation) and a lighter workout during the post-ovulatory phase.

Again, everything is related to the distinct individual situation: how you react to your menstrual cycle.

However, what matters is the will that one has or can acquire.

=== Woman and Fitness ===

Female biotypes

By biotype, we mean a particular body constitution characterized by common morphological and functional characteristics.

For women the main biotypes are:

The **Gynoid** has a "pear" shape, characterized by the accumulation of adipose tissue in the lower part of the body: hips, buttocks, thighs.

The **Android**, has an "apple" shape, with an accumulation of adipose tissue in the upper part of the body: shoulders, arms, abdomen, breasts, neck, chest

The **Mixed** biotype, has a "pepper" shape characterized by the combination of the two previous characteristics.

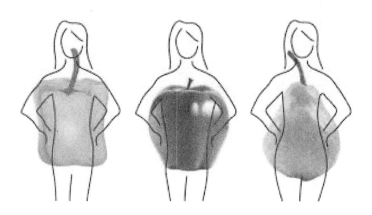

Understanding which biotype one belongs to can be useful for establishing a training path that targets the deficient areas and leads to improving your general appearance. Unfortunately, we do not lose weight selectively, so if fat accumulates on the hips and buttocks, it is useless to concentrate especially on that area. It is most useful to adopt a strategy that leads to an increase in metabolism rate, capable of moving fat, but always combined with the right diet.

=== Woman and Fitness ===

Water retention

With "water retention" we indicate the tendency to retain fluids in the body. Generally, it is an accumulation of liquids in the spaces between cell and cell. Fluid stagnation is usually found in areas prone to fat accumulation (abdomen, thighs, buttocks, knees, and ankles). The result is an abnormal inflammation caused by a venous and lymphatic circulation not properly functioning. Often there is a tendency to attribute one's overweight state to water retention but, if we exclude the case of kidney or cardiovascular diseases or abnormal levels of estrogen or cholesterol, the opposite is true: overweight, excess of fat, contributes to water retention and its physical manifestations.

The causes are as usual a result of bad eating habits and a too sedentary lifestyle. There are no magic pills or secrets to having the physique of your dreams: you need to move your body more.

If water retention is given by the stagnation of liquids between cell and cell, it is necessary to understand how liquids are managed in the human body. In this context, the quantities of sodium (salt) and potassium play a key role.

Over half of your body weight is composed of water. The water in the body is concentrated in certain spaces, called compartments. The main compartments are:

Liquids inside the cells

Liquids in the space around the cells

To function normally, the body must ensure that the levels of liquids contained in these areas do not undergo excessive variations. Some minerals, especially **macrominerals** (minerals that the body needs in relatively large quantities) are important as **electrolytes**. Electrolytes are minerals that have an electrical charge when dissolved in a liquid, such as blood. Blood electrolytes - **sodium**, **potassium**, **chloride**, and **bicarbonate** - regulate nerve and muscle functions and maintain acid-base and water balance.

Electrolytes, particularly sodium, allow the body to maintain normal fluid levels in the compartments since the amount of fluid in a compartment depends on the concentration of electrolytes in it. If the concentration of **electrolytes** is high, liquids move to that compartment: this is the mechanism of cellular osmosis. Likewise, if the electrolyte concentration is low, liquids leave the compartment. To adjust the fluid levels, the body dynamically moves the electrolytes inside or outside the cells. Consequently, having the right concentration of electrolytes (electrolyte balance) is important for maintaining the balance of liquids between the compartments.

The kidneys help maintain electrolyte concentrations by filtering the electrolytes and water contained in the blood, returning part of it to the blood, and eliminating the excess amount through the urine. Therefore, the kidneys help maintain a balance between the daily intake and excretion of electrolytes and water.

Potassium is one of the body's electrolytes. Most of the potassium in the body is found inside the cells. Potassium is necessary for the normal functioning of cells, nerves, and muscles. The body must maintain blood potassium levels within very narrow limits. If the potassium level is too high (hyperkalemia) or too

=== Woman and Fitness ===

low (hypokalaemia), serious consequences can occur, such as altered heart rhythms or even cardiac arrest. The body uses the potassium contained within the cells to keep the potassium level in the blood constant. The body maintains the right level of potassium by balancing the amount introduced with the amount eliminated.

Aldosterone regulates the sodium/potassium ratio. Aldosterone is a steroid hormone produced by the adrenal glands. It regulates the volume of extracellular fluids, the volume of circulating blood, and the diameter of the arteries, causing vasoconstriction. In this way, it regulates blood pressure. Finally, it regulates the sodium/potassium ratio.

From what we have just seen, it is clear that excessive potassium intake will cause greater sodium retention by the body, blocking its elimination by the kidney and increasing water retention. The same happens with an insufficient intake of sodium: the body will always retain the amount it needs.

You have to balance the potassium intake based on sodium intake, drink a lot of water, or more water than you are usually used to. Just to give a reference, let's say 0.5 - 1 liter every 10 kg of lean mass (we will see later how to calculate lean mass). Eating more proteins, which have a diuretic effect and, when combined with the right training, allow for an increase in muscle mass and better control of water retention. Keep the salt taken in the diet between 0.5 and 1 g per liter of water drunk.

For potassium, adequate portions of vegetables and fruit will be sufficient. In any case, is better to reach a maximum ratio of 1:1 with the salt consumed.

There are no secrets: to improve your physical condition you need to introduce the right caloric quota and move your body more than you usually do. We will see in more detail in the following chapters the role of calories and the training methods most proper for change, for a body recomposition.

=== Woman and Fitness ===

Cellulite

Cellulite begins to manifest itself with the degeneration of the microcirculation of the adipose tissue, with consequent alteration of its metabolic functions. It is linked to what has been said for water retention: the presence and stagnation of liquids in the interstitial spaces of the cells that are not used correctly by the body for reasons related to the role of hormones and the poor blood flow that does not allow regular exchange cell metabolism in the areas where these problems occur most. In women, as mentioned, these areas tend to focus on the hips and buttocks. Besides, cellulite has an inflammatory component of the adipose tissue.

There are four **stages** of evolution of cellulite, I list them in order of severity:

Stage 1: An initial alteration of the blood microcirculation occurs. The vessels present an abnormal permeability of the wall and this causes exudation of the plasma, with stagnation and accumulation in the interstitial spaces. It is characterized by edema and can be considered a reversible state.

Stage 2: The phenomena that characterize the first stage increase. Microcirculation exchanges further decrease and there is also a stagnation of toxins. The skin becomes pale, cold, and pasty.

Stage 3: Micronodules are formed which further hinder metabolic exchanges, causing slow and progressive destruction of the connective tissue of the dermis. The skin has the classic orange peel appearance.

Stage 4: Micronodules become macronodules. An increase in fibrous tissue occurs as a response to inflammation of the surrounding tissue. The orange peel appearance of the skin becomes very pronounced, the skin is pale, cold, and painful. This stage can be considered irreversible.

Let's review the different types of cellulite.

Compact cellulite: it mainly affects subjects in good physical shape with little mobile tonic muscles. It is hard to the touch and is located on the knees, thighs, and buttocks.

Soft Cellulite: Typically affects people with hypotonic tissue, therefore middle-aged people, or people who change weight too quickly or are not balanced. It is located on the inside of the thighs and arms.

Edematous cellulite: It is associated many times with the compact one. It is characterized by the presence of liquid stagnation of the buttocks and pelvis, which gives the tissues a swollen and spongy appearance. It is often associated with the compact one. It is always associated with the poor venous and lymphatic circulation of the lower limbs.

From what has been said, we can say that cellulite is a progressive degeneration of the causes that lead to water retention. The solutions are the same, that is, those on which we can act: nutrition and physical exercise, with the aim, on the one hand, of stopping or reducing the production or enlargement of fat cells and on the other of improving blood circulation in the most important areas affected by water retention and cellulite.

=== **Woman and Fitness** ===

We will see in the next chapter what is and what is the role of adipose tissue, of fat mass.

=== Andrea Raimondi ===

Body Fat

In this chapter we will try to understand something more about body fat. We will focus later on lean mass, specifically on how to increase muscle hypertrophy, that is, on how to increase the volume of muscles. And how not to lose muscle tone while on a diet. This is the basis of body recomposition. Body fat or rather adipose tissue is made of particular cells called **adipocytes**. In humans, adipose tissue is of two types: *white adipose tissue* and *brown adipose tissue*. White adipose tissue is the most common in the human body. They take their name from the color they take when observed under an optical microscope. **White adipose tissue** (WAT) is made of unilocular fat cells, 50-100 microns large, and of a drop of triglycerides (chain of three fatty acids combined with a glycerol molecule) that occupies almost all of its space. The **brown adipose tissue** (BAT) is composed of multilocular fat cells, which do not have a single lipid drop but many small drops that increase the surface of fuel exposed to the cytosol. It is more available for cell metabolism, given the massive presence of mitochondria and the great vascularization. The brown adipose tissue has the sole *function of producing heat* because the mitochondria (cellular organelles involved in cellular respiration, i.e. the production of energy or heat) of the multilocular fat cells have fewer enzymes responsible for the production of energy and more enzymes and proteins responsible for the production heat. The number of cells in the adipose tissue varies from person to person: in thin individuals, they can be counted from 41 to 65 billion, in obese individuals they can reach 200 billion. The number of fat cells can increase or decrease. Their diameter varies from 70 to 120 micrometers (millionths of a meter). An adipose tissue cell is composed on average of 90% of lipids. Knowing that from a gram of lipids (fats) 9 kcal are obtained, we can easily calculate how many calories must be consumed to lose 100 grams of fat: 100 grams of fat tissue, contain 90% of lipids, therefore in our example, 90 grams. 90 * 9kcal = 810 kcal of energy. To lose 100 grams of fat you need to "burn" 810 kcal.

What is adipose tissue for?

The most evident role of adipose tissue involves the energy reserve function. The evolution of the human body over the millennia has meant that fat in women is deposited on the hips, thighs, and breasts while in men, especially in the abdomen and back. Probably the reasons lie in the female reproductive function: it has been seen that during the breastfeeding phase the fat deposited in those areas is more easily mobilized. It has been hypothesized the role that a certain physical conformation given by ideal ratios between waist and hips can attract the attention of men, we fall again into reproductive motivation. Moreover, if we look at things from the point of view of the human species, the main purpose of each of its members is to reproduce, to maintain, to guarantee the survival of the species as such. This is what happens in every form of life. The ability of the human brain to imagine and elaborate has led, over time, to the construction of mental superstructures that hide this simple truth: the conservation of the species. But let's get back to the fat. We mentioned earlier that the cells that form adipose tissue can grow both in size and in number, varying from person to person. We have seen that one gram of fat converts to about 9kcal, while one gram of carbohydrate converts to 4kcal. Furthermore, a maximum of about 500 grams of carbohydrates can be stored as an energy source, between muscles and the liver, in the form of glycogen.

If we take for example a woman of 60 kg with a percentage of fat of 25%, that is about the average, as the table inserted in the previous chapter shows, we get 15 kg of fat. We remove from these the part of essential fat, necessary for survival, which is 10-13% in women. In our example for convenience, we calculate 10% of the 60 kg of weight of our model: 6 kg of essential fat. In the end, we get 15-6= 9kg of fat that can be used as an energy source, that is 9kg * 1000 = 9000grams, which is 81,000 kcal. Estimating an average consumption of about 1,800 kcal per day, theoretically, the woman in our example could not eat for 45 days, assuming that all the energy comes from fat.

But why is energy stored in the form of fat? Because it is the type of tissue, of cells, that takes less space and provide, as we have just seen, double the amount of energy compared to carbohydrates and proteins. Each gram of stored glycogen brings with it 3-4 grams of water, while the triglycerides of water only need about one gram.

Another important role of the fat mass concerns the protective function of the internal organs and the function of isolating from the external temperature, especially from the cold. Adipose tissue plays an important role in the overall regulation of metabolism, releasing hormones and other compounds that act on other tissues, such as the brain, liver, and skeletal muscle. It plays a role in glucose metabolism, blood pressure, appetite, hormone production. Among these, we find, for example, leptin which plays a role in appetite management, angiotensin II which plays a role in blood pressure control, the anabolic hormone IGF1, or the production of cytokines, involved in the immune system.

Therefore body fat should not be seen only as an enemy that we carry with us. It brings important tasks for the well-being of the person. The point is not to reach food overdoses.

There are four types of fat based on their location and type of cells, we briefly describe them:

Essential fat is found around the organs, with a protective role, in the nervous system, enveloping the nerves, and especially in the brain. Fat of this type is necessary for the body to maintain its normal functions and can be considered the maximum limit that can be reached by a weight loss process. We have already seen that the percentage of essential fat is higher in a woman (9-12%) than in a man (3%).

Brown adipose tissue, whose main role is to use energy, mainly to heat the body. It is mainly composed of mitochondria, which can use fatty acids to produce heat. The human body is endowed with it in limited quantities, so it is not this type of fat that we must aim for if we want to lose weight.

Visceral fat is found in contact with internal organs, below the muscles, especially in the abdominal area. It is a metabolically active fat, better supplied by the bloodstream, which allows it to be reduced more easily as a result of the correct stimuli, both in food and above all through aerobic workouts. Probably because anaerobic training increases the release of catecholamines, which has been shown to act more on the metabolism of this type of fat. **Subcutaneous fat** is found, as the name implies, under the skin. It is the type of fat that we try to eliminate with nutrition and training. Of all body fat, 40% to 60% is found under the skin. The distribution of this fat varies between men and women. For women it is located mainly on the hips, thighs, and breast area, generating the biotypes seen in previous chapters. Hormones play a fundamental role in the distribution of visceral and subcutaneous fat: during menopause, by decreasing the production of estrogen, there is usually an increase in abdominal visceral fat, which is typical of men. Not all subcutaneous fat has the same metabolic behavior: there is a difference between a thigh and hip fat and abdominal fat. Some research has even highlighted three different areas within the fat of the abdominal region: the deeper abdominal fat behaves like visceral fat and is relatively easier to eliminate; the more superficial abdominal fat has been divided into upper and lower, with the upper zone more easily eliminated than that of the lower zone. Fat of the hips and thighs is the most difficult to mobilize, partially for the reasons dealing with water retention. However, as in all matters that have to do with the human body, each person is different and reacts differently to the stimuli to which they are subjected, depending on their constitution and their metabolism.

=== Woman and Fitness ===

Fat cell metabolism

Four different metabolic events can occur in fat cells: **Hyperplasia**, the creation of new fat cells, which usually occurs in obese people. **Apoptosis**, the death, and disappearance of fat cells, an event that occurs only in certain conditions of extreme weight loss. **Lipogenesis**, formation of new fat in fat cells using glycerol and three free fatty acids. **Lipolysis**, the biochemical process contrary to lipogenesis, therefore the breakdown of fat in a cell of the adipose tissue to obtain glycerol and three free fatty acids.

Lipogenesis and lipolysis are processes that occur at the same time, we speak of the turnover of fat cells. The turnover varies according to the type of fat and is greater for visceral fat cells than for subcutaneous fat cells. From all this it is clear that there is a balance in the movement of fat cells: if the body stores more fat than is released, there is an increase in energy supplies and body weight.

Fat is composed of triglycerides already stored in adipose tissue. A source of triglycerides comes from dietary fat, the macronutrient that we will see in detail in the following chapters.

Once ingested and assimilated, dietary fat is broken down and inserted into the bloodstream about 3 hours later. A certain amount of ingested fat is used as an immediate energy source or ends up in the liver and skeletal muscle for energy function and to be stored in those organs; another portion goes in the cells of the adipose tissue to be potentially stored. In women it usually ends up in subcutaneous fat: some research has shown that when women eat, the body increases blood flow to the lower part, storing calories preferably in the hips and thighs.

Glucose is converted into glycerol in the fat cells that take it from the bloodstream, then joining it to the three free fatty acids that are already present in it to form the triglycerides that will be immobilized in the adipose tissue cell. Where does glucose come from? From carbohydrates ingested by eating, or from glycerol converted into glucose by the liver, or from some amino acids or pyruvate or lactate.

Some research has shown that the fat released by a cell is never stored in the same cell. There is a continuous exchange and rotation in the position of the various fatty acids, for which, for example, fatty acids released by the cells of the upper body terminate in the cells of the lower body and vice versa.

We can affirm that even if we introduce fat with the diet, we must always consider the total amount of kilocalories ingested: if we follow a low-calorie diet, that is, if we introduce fewer calories than those consumed during the week or month, the weight loss process will start or if you add more calories than you need to maintain a caloric balance, you will experience an increase in fat mass.

=== Woman and Fitness ===

Fat burning

Burn the fat

What does it mean to "burn" fat? It means nothing, the process by which fatty acids are used to produce energy is called oxidation because the biochemical reactions that take place use oxygen. At the end of the process, these biochemical reactions produce adenosine triphosphate ATP, which is the only source of energy for the cells. The triglycerides of the adipose tissue are used, through their fatty acids, to produce ATP by the cells of the body. Few tissues, including the brain, do not use fatty acids directly for energy, although they can use the ketones produced by the liver from fatty acids. For triglycerides used by cells, a process must take place which theoretically breaks down into three parts: a *breakdown* into three fatty acids and a glycerol molecule, *transport* of fatty acids into the bloodstream utilizing a protein, albumin, and *use by the cells* that employ them to produce energy through the mitochondria or to make new triglycerides, in the liver or muscles. Its usage as an energy source depends on the level of some enzymes. The enzyme level controls the level of glycogen in the muscles: the higher this level, the lower the oxidation of fats. To *increase* the oxidation of fats, glycogen must be used in the muscles, through training. To improve its transport into the bloodstream, aerobic activity can be used. Returning to the first step that must be carried out by triglycerides, the breaking of the bond between the three fatty acids and glycerol, this process is mainly driven by the level of an enzyme called **HSL**, hormone-sensitive lipase. Many other hormones are involved in its level, including testosterone, cortisol, estrogen, GH, but above all the levels of *catecholamines* and **insulin**. Insulin acts as an HSL inhibitor, insulin aims to keep blood sugar levels stable in the bloodstream, intervening every time you eat something to compensate for the rise in blood glucose levels. We can deduce that every time you eat, the use of fatty acids as an energy source is blocked. Catecholamines, adrenaline, and noradrenaline, on the other hand, increase the activity of HSL, interacting with catecholamines through adrenoceptors positioned on the surface of the cells. Adrenoceptors can be of type α (alpha) and type β (beta). A receptors are located on the surface of intestinal, skin, and kidney smooth muscle cells. The binding of adrenaline to these α receptors induces arterial contraction by reducing the blood flow in the affected organs. B receptors are found on the surface of liver, fat, and heart cells. The binding of adrenaline to the β receptors increases the rate of contraction of the myocardium, increasing blood perfusion to other tissues. The stimulation of β receptors increases levels of circulating essential fatty acids allowing their use as an energy source. Not many β-type receptors are found in the subcutaneous fat of the hips and thighs, which contributes to making this fat more difficult to remove.

Anyway, insulin prevails over other reactions because it has the most important role, that is to maintain the quality of blood stable. Furthermore, it must be considered that the body tends to conserve stored energy to allow the body to survive in periods of food scarcity. The body store this energy, in the form of triglycerides, on every occasion it can, at every meal.

From this quick and simplified look at the functioning of cell metabolism, we can draw the following conclusions: we can intervene on this metabolism in two ways: with nutrition and with exercise. This is especially true for women who, for sociological and practical reasons, move less than men and practice less sport, especially in adulthood. Thus losing one of the two pillars on which the maintenance of a body without fat is based: physical activity. So it is not so important how much you eat but how much you consume.

In the next chapters, we will deepen both the aspects related to nutrition and those related to training.

=== Andrea Raimondi ===

=== Woman and Fitness ===

Energy systems

How does the human body produce the energy to live and to contract muscles?

All life forms need energy to grow, move and maintain. Thousands of energy-requiring processes continually occur within cells to meet life's demands. Energy can take many forms in biological systems, but the most useful energy molecule is known as adenosine triphosphate (ATP).

There are four different energy systems that generate ATP during exercise. In the context of physical activity, the contribution of each of these systems is determined by its intensity and duration. The four energy systems of the body are:

the **anaerobic alactacid** system or phosphagen system, with the use of energy substrates such as adenosine triphosphate (ATP) and phosphocreatine (PC);

the **anaerobic lactacid** or glycolysis system, with the use of energy substrates such as glycogen and glucose, given by carbohydrates;

the **aerobic glycolytic** system, with the use of energy substrates such as glycogen / glucose;

the **aerobic lipolytic** system with the use of energy substrates such as free fatty acids (FFA).

We note here that the use of the source constituted by body fats is activated following a prolonged, and not maximal, effort. From this fact derives the importance of aerobic training sessions in case you need to lose weight. For this purpose it is useful to adopt training techniques such as the so-called "circuit" one, which allows you to increase oxygen consumption during training. However, we always keep in mind that all energy systems work simultaneously to produce or restore energy supplies. The muscle fiber cell transforms chemical energy into movement by means of muscle contraction. Chemical energy derives from the degradation of ATP. The duration of muscular effort forces the cells to run out of immediately usable stocks and to resort to other sources such as glucose, through the mechanism of glycolysis. This mechanism leads to the formation of lactic acid, which in turn sets in motion a series of reactions in the cellular environment that lead to curb the production of ATP itself. At this point, oxygen comes into play, which is able to degrade glucose with greater efficiency. Oxygen is carried from the outside of the muscle fiber cells through the blood. In this way, slow-twitch red fibers are preferred, which are more charged with blood, and therefore with oxygen, and allow the effort to be prolonged for even long times, but not at the maximum level. The speed with which ATP is rebuilt allows the muscle contraction to continue. Exercise produces the necessary adjustments to improve this mechanism.

The energy needed by the body, we have seen, comes from food consumption. The body's cells can use various types of fuel. The fuel used mainly and in normal conditions is produced by the breakdown of carbohydrates and fats, while in extreme cases only, proteins are degraded. We will see later in more detail what these elements are, and what they do. For the moment it is im-

=== Woman and Fitness ===

portant to understand how power can be used to improve energy supply.

Carbohydrates and energy

Carbohydrates or glycides or sugars are the first form of energy that all cells use in normal conditions and during physical exercise.

The carbohydrates present in food have different constitution, some are simpler, others have a more complex structure. The latter are transformed through digestion into simpler compounds, until glucose is obtained.

Glucose is present in foods of vegetal origin or is produced in the intestine by obtaining it from complex carbohydrates such as disaccharides (like lactose present in milk, for example), oligosaccharides or polysaccharides, such as starches.

Once produced, glucose is transported through the blood to all the tissues that use it, or it is stored in the form of glycogen in the liver and muscles.

If glucose production exceeds the capacity for use and storage, its molecules are transformed into fatty acids and stored in adipose tissue. This process occurs both directly in the liver and in the tissues, mainly in the adipose tissue.

Glucose is also the main energy source for the brain and for red blood cells.

A minimum amount of glucose is always produced from proteins in cases of absolute lack of other source. Anyway, the glucose storage capacity is limited, and prolonged exercise leads to

[37]

rapidly depleting its stores. In this case, glucose must be produced using chemical processes mediated by oxygen.

The intake of carbohydrates triggers the biochemical reactions that serve to make glucose available. These reactions are driven by a series of hormones.

One of the most important is **insulin**. This protein hormone, once produced, has an average life of 7-15 minutes in the blood and its secretion is regulated by blood sugar levels and by the concentration of glucagon. **Glucagon** is a hormone produced by the pancreas and its role is opposite to that of insulin: insulin has a hypoglycemic activity, that is, it lowers blood sugar, while glucagon has a hyperglycemic activity, that is, it increases the production of glucose. Insulin inhibits the lipolysis process (use of fatty acids in order to produce energy), increasing the fat storage process.

In a healthy person, when blood glucose levels drop below the threshold of about 80mg/100ml, the pancreas secretes glucagon, which leads to the production of glucose through the use of glycogen stores. They are stored in the liver and muscles. However, when glucose levels are high, the glucagon level is reduced and glycolysis is activated. Insulin stimulates the use of glucose by all the tissues that depend on it. The use of glucose ensures that situations of hyperglycemia do not occur. At the same time, the synthesis of fatty acids and their storage in the adipose tissue through triglycerides are stimulated.

It also increases, thanks to the stimulation of insulin, protein synthesis in all tissues, counteracting proteolysis, the use of

=== Woman and Fitness ===

amino acids for energy purposes; combined with the action of other hormones, it therefore promotes the muscle growth process.

In general, we can say that insulin can promote an increase fat mass when in the prevalent presence of carbohydrates, while it can favor the process of increasing lean mass in the prevalent presence of proteins.

In general, we can say that the intake of carbohydrates is best accompanied by other macronutrients, such as fibers or fats, which reduce excessive increases in insulin, delaying, with their presence, the speed of sugar absorption. From this comes the advice, which is often heard, to use wholemeal bread and pasta, richer in fiber.

The duration and intensity of muscle action determines the source of energy used by the muscles. At rest, the main source used is given by fatty acids from adipose tissue. During moderate activity, the muscle can use fatty acids, glucose and ketone bodies produced by the liver.

Muscle action plays an important role in regulating the use of glucose provided by carbohydrates introduced with food. The muscles use about 80% of available glucose. Therefore, constant muscle activity, even if moderate, leads to an increase in insulin sensitivity, ensuring better absorption of glucose by the cells. And over time it leads to a reduction in fat mass and an increase in lean mass.

Protein and energy

Proteins can also be an energy source from their breaking down. However, this occurs in exceptional conditions, when adequate levels of carbohydrates or fats are not introduced with the diet and the body is subjected to prolonged physical effort. For this reason, it is necessary, in case of physical activity, to ensure an adequate supply of proteins, especially if you are looking for increases in muscle volume. Anyway, it is useless to overdo the intake of protein powder or in any other form.

Even if you want to build muscle mass, a proper diet, which uses more protein-containing foods, satisfies your muscle growth needs. Many food references that circulate in the wold of gym derive from athletes who use anabolics, which unnaturally stimulate muscle growth and need disproportionate amounts of protein to promote this process.

Protein intake for an adult is about 0.8-1.9 g. for kg of weight; it can go up to 1.5-2 g for kg of weight in phases of intense exercise for building muscle mass.

Fats and energy

Fats of the same weight have a much higher calorific value than carbohydrates and proteins. Fats dispense 9kcal / g, while carbohydrates and proteins around 4kcal / g. Furthermore, to be stored they do not need water and can be accumulated in a smaller volume. This property allows a consistent accumulation of fat in obese subjects.

=== Woman and Fitness ===

All cells have a small supply of fat, either built from dietary fat or made from sugars in excess. But the main source of fat for energy purposes is constituted by adipose tissue, which has the function of accumulating fat, as seen in the chapter dedicated to it. And it is from the adipose tissue that the body draws energy in periods of fasting, or particular conditions, such as during physical exercise. The use of fats for energy purposes changes, from the state of rest, in which it is found at 15%, to the energy requirement, to the conditions of marked and above all prolonged effort. In this case, fat consumption can reach half the energy requirement. We can say that the longer the exercise and the more intense the effort, the more fats are recruited as an energy source. The parameter used to evaluate the type of energy source used is the **Respiratory Quotient** (R.Q.), which is obtained from the following equation: $R.Q = CO_2$ emitted / O_2 inspired. The more this parameter approaches 1, the greater the use of sugars; on the other hand, a value close to 0.7 indicates an almost exclusive use of fats for energy production. The R.Q at rest is on average 0.8, therefore fat is consumed more (68% and 32% carbohydrates). The more a person trains, the more this ratio approaches 0.7; a sedentary instead tends towards the ratio of 1. This highlights the fact that the sedentary subject will tend not to use the stores of fat as an energy source, and therefore to accumulate more and more of it (relative to how many kcal are introduced with the diet). The increase in the use of fats as an energy source essentially depends on the fact that carbohydrates, i.e. sugars, can only be stored in limited quantities in the organs, in the form of glucose, and are quickly exhausted during prolonged muscular effort.

=== Woman and Fitness ===

Kilocalories

In thermodynamics, the calorie (or small calorie, symbol cal) is a unit of measurement of energy.

It was originally defined as the energy needed to raise the temperature of 1 g. of distilled water at atmospheric pressure by 1 ° C (precisely, from 14.5 ° C to 15.5 ° C).

In common parlance, the word "calories" generally refers to kilocalories: by saying that in a pound of bread there are 250 calories, for example, we mean 250 kilocalories (or 250,000 calories proper).

In biology and nutrition the kilocalorie (symbol kcal), or large calorie (symbol Cal), is the energy needed to raise the temperature of 1 kg of distilled water at a pressure of 1 atm by 1 ° C, and therefore corresponds to 1,000 small calories. It is used to indicate the average energy intake of a certain specified amount of food (such as one gram, 100 grams or one serving). Although the energy value of a food and the consumption of energy in physical activity are still indicated in Cal (or kcal), the International System of Units adopts the joule (J) and its multiple kilojoule (kJ, equal to 1,000 J).

The determination of the caloric intake was initially made for the simplest sugar, glucose, the easiest food to assimilate. Taking into account that 1 g of carbohydrates develops 3.8 kcal, 1 g of protein 4 kcal and 1 g of lipids 9.3 kcal (and 1 g of alcohol 7 kcal) of each food, the average energy intake can be determined on the basis of its components. The average calorie intake is in-

[43]

=== Andrea Raimondi ===

dicated on the packaging of almost all foods, typically expressed in kcal / 100 g

The most important thing in using the calculation of kilocalories concerns the fact that they represent a yardstick that allows us to define the starting point where we are, before starting a weight loss or body recomposition process.

Knowing the kcal that we have to introduce with a given diet, we can, using food labels, create a food plan, freeing ourselves from the food trends of the moment. Nutritional labels report the content in grams of macro elements, allowing us to know what we are actually eating. In the following example, referring to milk:

Nutrition Facts

8 servings per container

Serving size   **1 cup (240 mL)**

Amount Per Serving

Calories   150

	% Daily Value*
Total Fat 8g	**10%**
Saturated Fat 5g	**25%**
Trans Fat 0g	
Cholesterol 30mg	**10%**
Sodium 120mg	**5%**
Total Carbohydrate 12g	**4%**
Dietary Fiber 0g	**0%**
Total Sugars 11g	
Includes 0g Added Sugars	**0%**
Protein 8g	**16%**
Vitamin D 0mcg	**0%**
Calcium 390mg	**30%**
Iron 0mg	**0%**
Potassium 357mg	**8%**

* The % Daily Value (DV) tells you how much a nutrient in a serving of food contributes to a daily diet. 2,000 calories a day is used for general nutrition advice.

INGREDIENTS: Organic Whole Milk

=== Woman and Fitness ===

Energy balance

Life in general relies on consuming energy to carry out any activity. The energy expended must be replenished. This is true starting from the microscopic level, that of the cell.

If you want to increase muscle mass, to generate more muscle cells, it is necessary that the body has the elements and energy sufficient for this purpose, and that this excess energy is used for muscle building and not set aside as energy reserve. For this, first of all, a stimulus is needed so that muscle growth can take place. This growth drive is produced by sensible training aimed at hypertrophy, in this case.

Ultimately, it is the presence of a positive energy balance between intake and consumption that promotes muscle growth through exercise. The right amount of energy is needed. This is another factor that make bodybuilding a "scientific art".

At the molecular level, the caloric restriction protracted for a certain time, which varies from individual to individual, triggers a series of synthesis processes that result in a decrease in protein synthesis and, after a certain threshold, on the basis of homeostatic needs of the human body, it can lead to processes of catabolism (destruction of resources) that limit the increase in muscle fibers, both in number and in size.

Conversely, a greater availability of energy and therefore of nutrients allows and stimulates the anabolic process of growth.

Of course, constant exercise and a caloric surplus is necessary that is in line with an increase in training effort, in order not to significantly increase the adipose layer compared to the lean mass.

In this sense, knowing your energy balance plays an important role, starting from knowing how many kilocalories you consume in a day or a week.

For this purpose, over the years, various methods of calculating energy consumption have been proposed, with related mathematical formulas. These formulas are based on some parameters: weight, height, age, level of activity.

The aim is to arrive at the definition of the amount of calories to be consumed necessary to maintain the same level of activity, without gaining weight or losing weight.

This energy consumption can be expressed through the **TDEE** (Total Daily Energy Expenditure). It represents the total number of calories burned on a given day, and is the sum of four factors:

- Basal metabolism
- Thermal effect of food
- Activity thermogenesis not caused by training
- Thermal effect of training

Basal metabolic rate (BMR) can be derived from the following formula:

Female BMR

655 + (9.6 x weight in kg) + (1.8 x height in cm) - (4.7 x age in years)

Male BMR

66 + (13.7 x weight in kg) + (5 x height in cm) - (6.8 x age in years)

Multipliers are then applied to the calories of the basal metabolic rate to approximate the other items which constitute the TDEE. These multipliers are based on the level of daily physical activity performed by an individual.

The practical utility of calculating this parameter lies not so much in its scientific accuracy, but rather in the fact that it allows you to *define a starting point* on which base the strategy to achieve the goals, whether they are weight loss or muscle mass gain.

Then, scientifically, we will be able to manipulate the components of nutrition and physical exercise to increase or decrease the calorie intake and/or energy consumption, to achieve the expected results.

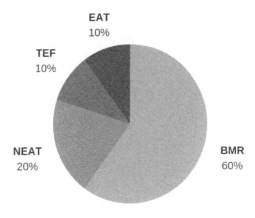

=== Andrea Raimondi ===

Food categories

From a biological point of view, the human organism is a system that exchanges substances, that come mostly from food, with the environment in which it lives.

Like all living beings, the human species needs to eat to live, in an incessant exchange of energy and matter.

To keep a body alive there must be a balance between energy expenditure and supply. By means of food we get all the chemical compounds that the body needs. These chemical compounds are nutrients, molecules introduced into the body through food and which undergo various biochemical processes to be then used by the various physiological processes.

Food sciences have identified 45 elements defined as essential, without which, life would not be possible. Thanks to bromatology, the science that studies the chemical composition of foods, we know what the various foods are made of. This has allowed, on one side to divide them into certain categories, having similar characteristics, and on the other to understand their chemical composition.

No food has brought together all the elements we need to live, there is no complete food. For this, it is essential to know their composition to create an optimal diet plan, in view of achieving a better physical state.

The nutritional profiles of the various foods allow them to be divided into 7 categories.

A diet that uses components of all 7 categories, guarantees the intake of the essential elements for proper nutrition. At least in chemical terms, because the quantity introduced must always be considered with respect to the needs of the organism.

category 1: meat, fish and fishery products, eggs

This category combines foods that come from the animal world. It is a source of amino acids, minerals (potassium, phosphorus, magnesium), microelements (zinc, copper, iodine, selenium) and some vitamins (B1, B2, B3, B6, B12). They may also contain sodium and fat. As for proteins, it must be remembered that not all foods in this category provide the same essential amino-acids and in the same quantities. In this context, "biological value" is used, distinguishing proteins based on the quantity of essential amino-acids that compose them. For example, Proteins derived from mammals have a greater biological value than those derived from poultry, eggs and fish.

category 2: milk and derivatives

In this category we can find proteins of high biological value and it is essential for the contribution of calcium, phosphorus and vitamins B2, A, D and E. There are also other elements to a negligible extent to cover the needs of an adult person.

category 3: cereals

Cereals represent an important energy source, in particular for the starch (which is a type of sugar), for the fiber and for some minerals such as iron, chromium, zinc, copper.

category 4: legumes

They represent a source of protein, even if not of high biological value, because they lack essential amino-acids such as methionine. They are also a source of starch, fiber, minerals such as iron, potassium, magnesium and some vitamins.

category 5: lipids or fats

They can be both solid and liquid, like oils. They are an energy source and also facilitate the transport of some vitamins (the fat-soluble ones) and essential fatty acids (omega 3 and 6).

category 6: vegetables

Category rich in water, minerals, sugars, vitamins, especially vitamins C and A and provide a large fiber content.

category 7: fruit

Category with the same elements as vegetables but with a higher quantity of sugars, especially fructose.

A separate category is given by **alcohol** which essentially represents an energy source due to the amount of sugar it contains.

=== Andrea Raimondi ===

Macronutrients

Together with the energy balance, it is important to identify the right subdivision of macronutrients.

Macronutrients are divided into:
- Proteins
- Carbohydrates
- Lipids

They provide the compounds necessary for survival, compounds from which the body obtains the energy it needs to perform its numerous functions, both voluntary and involuntary.

The main energy source of the human body is made up of carbohydrates (different types of sugars or fibers). Carbohydrates are the body's preferred source of energy as it is the least expensive to obtain through digestive biochemical processes.

During digestion, the so-called complex carbohydrates, because they are made up of more than one molecule, are broken down into the various types of monosaccharides by digestive enzymes, and then absorbed in the form of glucose.

With the increase in the amount of glucose in the blood, the endocrine system responds by increasing the glycemic response, introducing a quantity of insulin into circulation that is able to restore the system in balance. Through the **Glycemic Index** (GI) we have a measure of the speed with which a food causes an increase in blood glucose. In this way, foods with high, medium and low GI are distinguished. With high GI we have, apart from glucose, white bread, potatoes, cereals, grapes, bananas, carrots. With medium GI, we find wholemeal bread, pasta, corn, brown rice. With low GI, we have fructose, yogurt, peas, apples, peaches.

The body uses glucose directly as an energy source in the muscles, brain, and other cells. For this reason carbohydrates represent the main energy source: because it is the one most easily obtainable by the body, because it is obtained directly with the absorption of monosaccharide carbohydrates in small intestine. They are then inserted into the bloodstream to the cells that require them, and, through appropriate transformations, they can be converted into glycogen and stored in the liver and muscles as a rapidly available source of energy. A caloric surplus can also be retained in the body as an energy reserve in form of fat (triglycerides). These energy reserves will be used in absence of an adequate supply of sugars.

Carbohydrates provide about 4 Kcal. per gram, as stated before.

Proteins perform a structural and also energetic function by providing 4Kcal. per gram. They are present both in foods of animal origin, mostly of high biological value, and of vegetable origin, which are proteins of medium or low biological value. Proteins are molecules formed by the combination of twenty amino acids, nine of which are defined as "*essential*", because the body is unable to produce them. They are:

phenylalanine
isoleucine
histidine
leucine

lysine
methionine
threonine
tryptophan
valine

Among the essential amino acids, there are three branched ones: isoleucine, leucine and valine. These have the particularity of being picked up directly by the muscles, without passing through the liver, where they can then be used to repair damaged protein structures or to produce energy.

Proteins also perform structural function of building and / or repairing damaged tissues, also for this reason it is important to ensure an adequate protein intake, if you want to increase muscle mass. We must not forget their role in muscle contraction and in the transport of substances between one cell and another or within individual cells.

Fats like proteins have different roles within the body, for example they provide energy (9Kcal. per gram) and, in the form of triglyceride cells, act as reserve energy. Fats also have a structural function because they are components of cell membranes and are part of the substances that cover fibers. The adipose tissue acts as a thermal insulator for the body, and they are also essential for the absorption of fat-soluble vitamins such as vitamins A, D, E, K. The lipids that are most important from a nutritional point of view are: triglycerides, accumulated in the cells deposit; phospholipids, constituents of the cell membrane and sheaths of nerve fibers; cholesterol, a component of many hormones and is part of cell membranes.

It is good to reiterate the concept that the macronutrients taken in excess, since they cannot be stored directly in the body, are transformed into sugars which, in turn, are transformed into fats (triglycerides). If the latter are not consumed by the body, they will increase adipose deposits.

The various procedures that take the name of "**body recomposition**" are nothing more than methods that cycle the intake of carbohydrates, combining them with a specific workout, in an attempt to push the body to use fat as a source of energy supply.

These procedures must have a certain duration over time, usually longer than three weeks, and require a minimum carbohydrate intake of 40-50 grams per day, while increasing the intake of proteins and fats.

We often hear talking, in the environments of gyms, of **nutrient timing**, that is, when to take proteins or other macronutrients to maximize their effect on hypertrophy. There is currently no definite scientific evidence on this topic, so the general rule applies, in case of weight loss or muscle definition, must have to create a caloric deficit to decrease body fat deposits, favoring an adequate intake of proteins.

Even with regard to the integration chapter, the most disparate theories are often heard. We must never forget that we live in a society based on commodities. Integration is an industry that must constantly find and renew its outlet markets, often inducing needs that are not actually useful for weight loss or body recomposition.

Integrating means adding and, as can be understood by studying human biochemistry and physiology, everything the body needs to grow is found or built through **proper nutrition**. Everything that goes beyond physiological needs pass through the body's waste processes. This also applies to an excess of protein or vitamin or other component.

The only supplement that can guarantee certain results is given by the use of substances such as **steroids** that lead to changes in the normal functioning of the endocrine glands, thus leading to the formation of muscle masses that cannot be obtained with simple exercise and nutrition.

There is no scientific evidence, for the moment, that establishes whether a given element has a precise effect on weight loss or mass supply, other than, for example, in case of protein powders, to increase protein intake without having to eat kilograms of meat.

What is certain is that the use of overloaded exercise over time leads to an increase in muscle mass.

Having a body of a certain type, as proposed by magazines and social media, depends, with the same training and all other conditions, on individual genetics: on how much your biochemical system responds to the production of hormones, on the type of muscle fibers and the bone conformation of each subject.

If you want to overcome your genetic limits, you have to resort to substances that alter this natural constitution. This has been done and is regularly done by those who have made their body the source of their livelihood: bodybuilding champions, models, actors, fall in this category.

This is not meant to be a moralistic discourse, on the contrary I believe that everyone is free to experiment with their own body or on their body as they want, if this practice does not harm other people.

In many books, an intake of creatine, protein powder and some microelements, such as vitamins, and fatty acids, such as omega 3 is indicated as optimal or even necessary.

The only truth is that without continuity and adequate training for muscle development and without the right diet, no results are obtained. Integration integrates, in fact, and it is often only a psychological question of self-suggestion that a given substance can "push" more. Most of the time it's just a question of marketing.

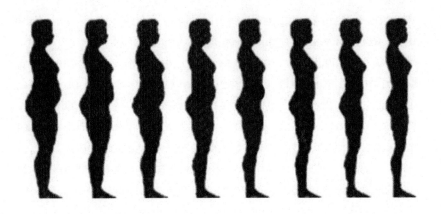

=== Woman and Fitness ===

Micronutrients

Vitamins and **minerals** are part of this group of nutrients. Micronutrients play both a structural and functional role. Based on their concentration, they are divided into macro and micro minerals. Their action takes place essentially at the cellular level, playing a role in the muscle contraction mechanism. It is the exchange of charges between positively charged ionized minerals and negatively charged ionized minerals that allows muscle contraction.

Among the *macrominerals* we have:
Calcium, the main source of which is milk, cereals, meat and fish, and drinking water.
Phosphorus is found in legumes, milk, foods that provide proteins, therefore meat, eggs.
Magnesium, especially in legumes and nuts, whole grains.
Sodium, cooking salt, sausages, and cheeses.
Potassium, especially from fruits and vegetables.

Among the *microminerals*
Zinc, the main sources are meat, fish, eggs and milk and derivatives and cereals
Copper, found in shellfish, crustaceans, and dried fruit
Iron, in foods of animal origin
Iodine, especially in sea fish and crustaceans but also in eggs, milk, and meat

[59]

Selenium, contained in foods of marine origin, dried and oily fruit, eggs, also in fruits and vegetables

Chromium, especially in cereals, egg yolk, some meats, some vegetables

Fluorine is bound to proteins or in the form of fluoride in water.

Role of water

Water is a fundamental nutrient for our body. The human body is mainly composed of this element which accounts for about 60% of a person's weight. It is found both inside and outside the cells. There is a continuous replacement of water that must be introduced with the power supply. All foods, especially fruit and vegetables, contain water, except for oil and refined sugar. There is therefore a water balance that requires, in normal cases, to consume at least 1.5 liters of water every day. *The advice is to drink 0.5 - 1 liter of water for every 10 kg of lean mass.* We will see in the next chapters how to calculate lean mass. The consumption of water plays an even more important role for women because it allows a greater exchange and change of intracellular and extracellular fluids, allowing to compensate for any sodium (salt) overdose and help to recover the problem of water retention, as we have seen in the chapter dedicated to it.

=== Woman and Fitness ===

Supplements

Proper nutrition ensures the right amount of macro and microelements needed by the body. Only in cases of lack of a given element it is advisable to supplement it: in people with pathologies, or in situations where the body is pushed beyond a normal balance.

One of these cases could concern who are committed to increasing muscle mass, using protein intake.

All types of supplements on the market, unless they are anabolic steroid, do not bring sensitive benefits to body recomposition. They don't make you lose weight, they don't increase your muscles.

To lose weight, a low-calorie diet is necessarily required, that is, one that leads to a caloric intake lower than energy consumption. Supplements are commodities and as such must be sold in some way, often using, to support them, incomplete data or not sufficiently validated by scientific research. It is also common to most of us to think that there is a magic pill, capable of solving problems simply and quickly. Unfortunately this is not the case.

Creatine

Creatine is an amino acid that can be synthesized by the liver (1g/day), and is used in the muscles to regenerate ATP during the first few seconds of muscle contraction. This is why it is believed that it can improve efficiency during anaerobic performance with intense efforts. The human body can store a maximum of 0.3 g of it for every kg. of body weight. This fact alone would be enough to understand the limits of its supplementation.

However, there are no studies that unambiguously establish the precise role of its hiring. As always, the effect varies from person to person.

Carnitine

Carnitine is a short-chain non-protein amino acid that allows mitochondria to use fatty acids for the production of ATP.

In other words, carnitine is a transporter of long-chain fatty acids in the mitochondrial matrix, where fatty acids are converted into energy through the Beta-Oxidation process. So it may seem that it facilitates the use of body fat and leads to weight loss, but even in this case there are no studies that scientifically determine its effectiveness.

Protein powder

Here is the supplement most used by gym goers. They can be of animal or vegetable origin.

It allows you to increase protein intake more quickly and to reach the high protein levels required by a diet for muscle mass gain. It should be noted that without adequate effort, which leads, over time, to an increase in the body's protein requirements, a high protein intake only leads to an increase in their quantity eliminated via the kidney or intestine.

Multivitamin

In this case also, a higher intake of actual needs leads only to an increase in waste to be eliminated by the kidneys.

Omega 3

Omega-3s (or n-3 PUFAs) are a category of essential fatty acids (like omega-6s).

They are especially known for their presence in cell membranes and for maintaining the integrity of these membranes. They are present in fish and nuts. Used for their anti-inflammatory properties, they contribute to the normal functioning of the heart and the maintenance of normal cholesterol levels in the blood. They are also proposed for depression, high triglycerides, senile dementia, but there is no scientific evidence in this regard.

As already noted, that of supplements is an economic sector that needs to continuously expand its market and where competition is high, it is not surprising that particular properties of this or that element are often highlighted. Unless serious deficiencies or pathologies, with a correct and balanced diet, it is possible to provide the body with all the elements it needs to stay healthy and also to increase muscle mass. I refer you to my book "Bodybuilding and body recomposition" for a more in-depth discussion of the training phase necessary to gain muscle or lose weight by becoming stronger.

=== Andrea Raimondi ===

=== Woman and Fitness ===

Lean Mass

In the chapter dedicated to it, we dealt with fat mass and its metabolism. in the next chapters, we examine lean mass, mainly consisting of muscle tissue. It is important to combine the right caloric intake with physical exercise that strengthens the muscles, especially if you want to reshape your body. Also in this case, as for the diet, you should not be in a hurry: the results will come. The important factor is the correct planning of the training protocol, appropriate to the goal you want to achieve, as will be seen when we discuss the training variables and study the workouts I propose.

Homeostasis. This is the main feature of the human body, it is the tendency to maintain a constant condition, to ensure the survival of the human being. In seeking homeostasis, the body tends to save as much energy as possible in carrying out any type of bodily activity.

Any change in the external world that somehow affects the body activates mechanisms that seek, and under normal conditions, guarantee the return to the initial stage. Thus, when we introduce molecules in the form of food, the body begins a series of transformations, movements, and biochemical processes that aim to bring the body system back into a situation of equilibrium. Balance fundamental to life: think of the level of blood PH. It is constantly maintained at the optimal level through reactions and counter-reactions based on what we eat. Let's take for example the management of carbohydrates, which represent the main energy source, in the form of simple sugars, of our body: an excessive level of sugar in the blood triggers a whole series of biochemical reactions with the release of insulin which allows to stabilize the blood glucose level.

So, if you want to increase muscle mass and therefore change a previous state, you have to force the body to get out of homeostasis, you have to break the balance and reach a new level where the body has to have and manage a greater amount of muscle mass or lean mass.

This new level is reached through physical exercise. To maximize our efforts, physical exercise must not be done randomly but must be organized in such a way as to lead to the goal we have set for ourselves.

We will see in the rest of the book which are the variables that come into play and which are to be exploited to maximize the exercise aimed at hypertrophy, up to the proposal of a training plan that allows us to achieve our goal.

Of course, without constant practice and without accurately detecting what we do during a single workout, the distant the goal will remain. Or rather, we will not have comparative data that allow us to assess if we are going in the right direction. In no field like that of training, theory must be put into practice and verified in reality.

To get out of homeostasis, the body must therefore be subjected to stress that produces an adaptive response to the stress itself.

The neuromuscular system must be subjected to stress that overloads the initial capacity of the single muscle or muscle district. The response to this stress generates a series of neural and mus-

=== Woman and Fitness ===

cular adaptations. Neural improvements, that is efficiency in the execution of movements, manifest themselves over time by repeating the same movements. The repetition leads to an increasingly fluid execution and this leads, under adequate load stimuli, to hypertrophic muscle increases. In practice, muscle growth is produced by increasing the size and number of contractile proteins, actin and myosin, present in the muscle itself. These proteins are responsible for muscle movement. They form filaments that, during muscle contraction, slide over each other and, overlapping, cause the shortening of the myofibrils and, consequently, of the muscle fiber. Therefore at the base of the muscular contraction, there is the sliding of the actin filaments on those of myosin. The increase in muscle mass must be maintained over time because the body tends to save as much energy as possible and to eliminate components that are not used, such as muscles, which if not used consume energy anyway.

=== Andrea Raimondi ===

Muscle Physiology

We all have the idea that if stimulated continuously, the muscles grow in volume but few have the precise idea of what happens inside the muscle when it contracts.

Without going into too much detail if we contract a muscle, let's say the biceps, we notice a "fleshy" part, the muscular belly that is attached on both ends through tendons that keep the muscle anchored to the skeleton.

If we cut that muscular fleshy part right in the middle we will see a bunch of cord-like structures that make up the inside of the muscle belly called bundles. These bundles are made up of myocytes (muscle cells/fibers) which are long, thin, and run the full length of the muscle belly.

Within these myocytes are myofibrils which also run along their length. Myofibrils are simply a set of proteins that allow us to generate the force necessary to move the load while we train.

What interests us most is the classification of the types of existing muscle fibers; these are of two types called *type I fibers* and *type II fibers*.

Type I fibers, also called slow-twitch fibers, are resistant to fatigue and therefore suitable for activities that require greater muscular endurance. To reach the maximum tension of these fibers takes time and therefore they are not suitable for developing maximum strength. Type II fibers, also known as rapid contraction, because can be activated in a shorter time (we are always talking about milliseconds) and are recruited when an explosive force is needed. Unlike type I fibers they have less resistance. Under the microscope, they appear white while the type I fibers have a red color due to the presence of capillaries which explains their longer duration, being more oxygenated.

This subdivision into the types of fibers varies from muscle to muscle and from individual to individual.

Knowing the composition of the type of fibers in a muscle for a given individual is useful to be able to define more precisely how to train, i.e. whether to prefer a more prolonged (with greater sets and repetitions) or shorter duration (with higher loads).

Of course, it should not be forgotten that a muscle is composed of a mix of the two types of fibers and therefore it is necessary to understand which type of fiber is prevalent. It is necessary, through appropriate measurements, to understand if a muscle can bear a long and lighter work or a short and intense one.

The increase in muscle mass is essentially an adaptation to external stimuli imposed on the skeletal-muscular system through resistance training.

This adaptation leads to the improvement of nerve responses and an increase in the recruitment of muscle fibers. The human body is a machine built to save energy so initially, some contractile fibers are recruited. With the prolongation of the exercise, other fibers are activated and coordination between the various muscle groups is improved. All of this happens over time. The increase in muscle fibers or the increase in their size occurs thanks to a positive protein balance, given by the difference between how many proteins are destroyed and how many are synthesized through the diet. This is why it is advisable to introduce more protein in the diet if you intend to increase muscle mass.

We must say that introducing a greater amount of protein must be accompanied by increased activity otherwise the calories introduced in excess will be partly diverted to the energy reserves made up of fat cells, the triglycerides. Here, too, it is essential to coordinate the right diet with correct and subjective management of the training load. The aforementioned protein balance is conditioned to a certain extent by the neuroendocrine system, that is, by the production of certain hormones that can influence protein synthesis as a result of training stimuli. Among these, we have **IGF1**, a hormone similar to insulin, produced by muscle contraction. Another hormone that affects protein synthesis is the growth hormone (**GH**) which affects the functioning of IGF1, as well as Testosterone, by strengthening it. The latter is a hormone that acts directly on the increase of muscle mass, as shown by numerous studies. **Insulin** is also a hormone that plays a role in increasing muscle mass, although mostly on the side of the reduction of protein catabolism. In summary, it has been shown that physical exercise can increase the release of anabolic hormones and therefore muscle growth. I refer to specialized studies those who want to deepen this interesting topic, we are interested here in knowing that the right training and the right diet, in terms of calories introduced and type of macronutrients, pushes the body to adapt itself by increasing muscle mass and reducing (in case of caloric deficit) the fat component in the body.

Mechanisms of hypertrophy

Muscle tissue is mainly composed of water, about 70% and proteins about 25%. But it is the latter, as mentioned in the previous chapter, that allows the muscles to contract.

We must not think of our body as a static entity on a biochemical level: it is just the opposite.

Every moment the body breaks down molecules and reassembles them at the cellular level, the same goes for proteins.

It is the constant destruction and reconstruction of proteins thanks to the mechanisms that we will see in this chapter to allow the development and quantity of muscle development; that is, it depends on the balance between protein destruction and reconstruction.

If the balance is positive, new muscle mass will be built (anabolism), otherwise it will be impoverished (catabolism).

However, the process of muscle growth and protein growth does not take place in the training phase, when the muscle protein consumption is greater, but during rest.

After the training period (or muscle activation) it appears that protein synthesis (creation of new proteins) can remain active for 48 hours or more.

It is necessary to always keep in mind that when it comes to training or other aspects concerning human physiology, genetics plays a not secondary role in determining the biochemical response of the individual in the interaction with the environment, with the muscular effort imposed in our case.

=== Woman and Fitness ===

In order for the anabolic or catabolic protein process to be activated, there must be intracellular impulses with activation or suppression of certain substances and enzymes that interact within or between cells.

Concretely and visibly, the main mechanisms relating to muscle growth following physical activity are the following: muscle mechanical tension, metabolic stress and muscle damage.

We see them in more detail in the following paragraphs.

Mechanical Tension

The effort sustained by the muscles during training with loads is considered the main factor in their development. The stress undergone by the muscular system generates the phenomenon of mechanotransduction. It is the way by which mechanical movements are converted into chemical activity which in turn activate the anabolic processes.

Up to a certain threshold, the greater the load, the greater the adaptive response of the body.

This threshold also varies according to the time in which the muscles are under tension so you must always evaluate both the aspect of adequate load and the time of lifting the load, trying to find the right mix between the two factors.

In this case, also we must not think in one direction: when dealing with human physiology all the factors interact with each other.

Beyond that threshold, other mechanisms come into play that generates more strength, in a workout over the years, but not greater muscle growth.

Therefore, not only the load lifted is important in the training strategy for hypertrophy but also other factors must be taken into consideration to shape the training planning so it can be as productive as possible.

Metabolic Stress

It is a mechanism that occurs because of training. It produces an increase in the amount of water inside the trained muscle which leads to the activation of a set of chemical reactions that stimulate protein synthesis and the reduction of the breakdown of proteins.

Exercise leads to an increase in metabolites within the muscle such as lactate and inorganic phosphates. Some studies show that this mechanism is generated more as a result of anaerobic glycolysis which occurs with activities that last from 15 to 120 seconds.

This is what happens when you perform sets and repetitions that lead to muscle failure and therefore have sufficient duration to start the process described above.

To carry out an exercise of a certain duration, weights lifted must not reach the maximum. It is the technique used in bodybuilding in which you train not with maximum loads but with loads capable of making the sets last for 10-12 repetitions.

Some studies show that in this way all muscle fibers are activated through metabolic stress.

Metabolic stress induces hypertrophy through the production of anabolic myokines, a substance similar to hormones, with the increase in the amount of intracellular water and with the increase in anabolic hormones such as GH

Muscle Damage

It is caused by micro-tears in the muscle following intense exercise, caused by the breakdown of contractile proteins and the sarcolemma, the connective membrane that surrounds the muscle fibers. These tears activate the repair mechanism that starts the body's process of adapting to a future greater effort.

Although muscle growth is not always signaled by post-workout pain, because with the passing of experience the body adapts to the efforts and produces greater resistance to muscle pain, it has been hypothesized that muscle damage may be one of the causes of hypertrophy. Muscle damage leads to inflammatory processes and subsequent cellular repair through the accumulation of muscle proteins. The body would react to a stressful situation by producing more than is needed for a mere repair of the damage suffered, thus preparing the way for muscle growth.

To maximize muscle growth, a training methodology is needed that knows how to work with all these factors that lead to hypertrophy and weight loss, by managing their components correctly. From all this, it appears that it is not enough to base one's protocol on the increase of loads, which creates muscle damage. It is necessary to use the increase in mechanical tension, with the increase in the number of repetitions and the metabolic stimulus through the reduction of recovery between the various sets.

=== Woman and Fitness ===

Training Variables

=== Andrea Raimondi ===

=== Woman and Fitness ===

Volume

The **volume** parameter represents the total amount of work done in a training session, or over a certain period. It is defined as the sum of the repetitions performed during the training session, or rather as the sum of the repetitions performed with a certain load: n.set * n.reps * Kg load.

The greater the volume, the heavier a training session for the same time.For example, 3 sets of 10 repetitions with 50kg are equal to 1500kg of volume. Adding up the volume done for each exercise of a given session will give you the total volume of the session.

Studies confirm that greater volume produces greater metabolic stress and greater hypertrophic response.

Therefore, by modifying one of the parameters of volume, its quantity is changed. If it is true that, assuming to lift 10 kg, the same volume is obtained with 10 sets of 10 repetitions or with 5 sets of 20 repetitions, at the level of muscle fatigue is not the same thing. Because with more sets is greater the possibility of muscle recovery (with the same rest time between one set and another) and the metabolism can rebuild the energy consumed in the movement of muscles.

Therefore, in addition to the load, the duration of the recovery times must also be considered.

The **load** is the other variable that constitutes the volume and is a variable directly related to hypertrophy, as practically all studies show, greater load corresponds to greater development.

[79]

To create our training plans, we already have these variables available: the number of sets, the duration of the rest between one set and another, the number of repetitions, and the load.

There is an inverse physical correlation between the lifted load and the number of repetitions: the higher the load, the lower the number of repetitions. It is a trivial and obvious equation for everyone. The load with which we can perform only one repetition, using a correct joint movement, is indicated with 1RM, representing the maximum limit, the load capacity of a given person. Below this limit and therefore with lower loads we can perform more than one repetition.

In general, scientific and practical evidence states that to train strength you must use loads of 80-90-100% of 1RM, to train hypertrophy loads of 65% to 80% of 1RM.

To train **strength**: 85%-100% 1RM
To train **hypertrophy**: 65%-85% 1RM

Frequency

The frequency parameter indicates how many times the training sessions are carried out, usually taking the week as a reference. We can also talk about training frequency for a single muscle group when evaluating how many times a particular muscle group has been trained.

The microcycle represents the period within which all muscle groups are trained. For convenience, the duration of a week is also taken as a reference. In this time frame, we can define training days and rest days between workouts. Research has shown that higher training frequencies lead, all other conditions being equal, to improvements in muscle mass. It is often discussed which is the best frequency, what is ultimately the recovery time needed between one session and another to maximize hypertrophy. In recent years, some research has been produced on this topic but there is still no precise scientific evidence on the optimal duration of recovery between one workout and another: some researchers conclude the need to allow at least 48 hours to pass between one session and another. Other researchers say it would be better to wait at least 72 hours. Usually, the more or less pre-filled cards provide for 3 weekly workouts with one or more days of rest between workouts, especially in the case of **full-body** workouts. With this cadence, all the muscles of the body are trained at least three days a week. Or, for more advanced athletes, **split routines** are used in which not all muscle groups are trained in a single session but the muscles to be trained are separated, such as between muscles of the upper body and muscles of the lower body, being able in this way to increase the number of training sessions. A split routine allows also a greater variety of exercises for the trained muscles, for the same amount of time, compared to a routine that uses the full-body method. In any case, some authors highlight how resilience depends very much on the genetics of an individual. Again, several attempts and a greater scientific approach are needed to optimize efforts in terms of hypertrophy: not only affects the frequency with which you train but how you train, which muscles need more work because they tire less quickly, because they are mainly composed of slow-twitch fibers or because they have a greater recovery capacity.

=== Woman and Fitness ===

Load (Intensity)

Load is one of the main variables that generate muscle hypertrophy. It defines the weight in kilograms raised during the repetitions.

It is a variable based on the level of training of the subject and his strength and to be used in the preparation of the various training protocols it must be understood in a relative sense, as a percentage of the maximum load lifted in a given exercise, as a percentage of the 1RM. Indirectly provides a measure of the intensity of the effort sustained during training.

The maximum repetition is indicated with "**1RM**". Researchers formulated some hypotheses concerning the value of the maximum repetition without having to establish it directly by testing. Tables have been compiled that relate the number of repetitions performed with a given load to establish the maximum load of a subject.

If, for example, a maximum of 10 repetitions are performed with 50kg, based on the table I have entered below, this corresponds to 75% of 1RM so the maximum load of this person in that particular exercise should be 67 kg. Beyond the formulas used, which may change over time with new research or studies, the table is convenient for our purposes to create personalized training workouts thus providing a starting point to record the progress of our efforts towards the desired goals.

[83]

Correlation
between maximum repetitions and intensity
as a percentage of 1RM

100% 1RM = 1 maximum repetition
95% 1RM = 2 maximum repetitions
93% 1RM = 3 maximum repetitions
90% 1RM = 4 maximum repetitions
87% 1RM = 5 maximum repetitions
85% 1RM = 6 maximum repetitions
83% 1RM = 7 maximum repetitions
80% 1RM = 8 maximum repetitions
77% 1RM = 9 maximum repetitions
75% 1RM = 10 maximum repetitions
70% 1RM = 11 maximum repetitions
67% 1RM = 12 maximum repetitions
65% 1RM = 15 maximum repetitions
60% 1RM = 20 maximum repetitions

Type of Exercises

Varying the exercises is essential for muscle development because it allows you to train different parts of the muscle, especially for those muscles that have different insertion points on the skeleton. If we take for example the deltoid or the trapezius or the pectoral, these have different insertions and conformations such that they are more activated by performing a given movement. For the pectoral group, for example, the central areas of that muscle will be stressed more with the flat bench, while with the inclined bench the upper areas will be stressed more. In general, an area of the muscle is affected differently according to the movement of a given exercise.

One of the main distinctions in the type of exercise is between **multi-joint** and **single-joint** exercises.

The former involves several muscle groups during their execution because the movement involves several joints at the same time, while the latter involves only one joint. Multiarticular exercises such as the squat are usually more demanding on a systemic level and can be used more in those phases where greater metabolic activation is required.

Andrea Raimondi

Progression

Setting a progression in the training variables is essential to maximize the hypertrophic results of the training itself, always bearing in mind, however, that the right volume and load must be guaranteed during the training sessions. A progression concerns the change of one of the main training variables such as increasing the number of sets or repetitions or the load used between one microcycle and another or between one mesocycle and another.

For example, if in the first microcycle we held 3 sets for 12 repetitions using 15kg as maximum weight, in the following microcycle we can increase the sets, keeping the other parameters constant, so we will perform 5 sets for 12 repetitions with 15 kg, or we can increase the weight lift while holding the number of sets and reps, for example, we will do 3 sets for 12 reps with 17kg.

To check if you can maintain progression in your workouts, it is essential to keep a training diary in which we can write down exercises, loads, sets, repetitions, recovery times, and notes on the perception of effort. It will be possible to verify in practice whether our training is going in the desired direction.

TUT (Duration of Repetition)

TUT is the acronym for Time Under Tension, it indicates the duration of the muscle movement during a repetition. It is expressed in seconds.

If we think about the movement performed during a repetition, we notice that this can be broken down into 4 phases: a phase in which we move the weight by lifting it (called eccentric phase), a phase in which we reach maximum extension (or maximum contraction) and the movement stops (isometric stop) and then returns to the starting position by lowering the load (concentric phase), to finally stop the movement (isometric stop in shortened position) before starting the next repetition.

For each of these moments, it is possible to modify its duration: raising and lowering the load more slowly or faster, increasing or decreasing the duration of the pause between the two movements.

It is commonly used to express these four phases with figures such as 3141 which respectively indicate the duration in seconds of the eccentric phase, the duration of the stop in the extended position, the duration of the concentric phase, the duration of the stop in the shortened position.

Since there is no certain scientific evidence on the optimal time for the various phases of repetition, over time different schools of thought have been formed: there are those who affirm that it is the fast repetition that guarantees maximum muscle development and those who affirm the opposite, by aiming at a slow or very slow lift and return speed.

From our point of view, as for the other variables, it is necessary to experiment what is the best speed for a given person. In any case, it is essential to vary the stimuli in the various mesocycles from the point of view of the speed of execution also, keeping the only rule, to always keep a controlled movement and with execution as clean as possible, focusing on the muscle you are training.

We, therefore, have another arrow in our bow to try to stimulate muscle development and vary the stimuli to push the body to seek new homeostasis at a higher level than the previous one in terms of muscle mass.

Rest between Sets

Even with this training variable, it is possible to influence the results of muscle development because decreasing the pause time between one set and the next increases the metabolic stress and the hormonal and protein synthesis responses that we highlighted in the first chapter.

Therefore, with the same volume and intensity, minor pauses between sets lead to an accumulation of substances pro hypertrophy, but also a greater accumulation of fatigue.

The relationship between effort and fatigue must therefore be correctly measured. The experience in training and keeping track of the work done by noting the responses of one's body are highlighted using some physical parameters and some measurements, which we indicate in a subsequent chapter and can indicate the right mix between effort and fatigue for a given person.

=== Woman and Fitness ===

Training Techniques

We present here some specific methodologies for resistance training developed over the years by practice in the gym.

There are no studies that demonstrate which methodology is the best over another, but even in this case, we can use these techniques as a tool that we can use to produce variability in training.

The fact remains that to obtain an increased muscle mass you need time, consistency, and a training plan that guarantees the correct increase in training stimuli.

CIRCUIT TRAINING

Circuit training involves the execution of a certain number of exercises, completing a setss for each exercise and moving on to the next without rest between one setss and another. At the end of the established exercises, rest is performed. At the end of rest time resumes with the first exercise foreseen in the training plan. Canceling the rest between one exercise and another increases cardio-vascular work, increases metabolic stress and the aerobic phase. For these reasons it can be used in programs aimed at weight loss.

It can be used among others in the following ways:

• Organizing the entire training session in a single circuit to be repeated a set number of times.

[91]

- Setting the training session with 2 or more mini-circuits, perhaps divided by muscle areas.

PYRAMIDALS

Training with the pyramid method is based on the principle of providing an increase in the weight lifted with each set. The greater load and the fatigue that gradually accumulates in the trained muscle leads to a decrease in the number of repetitions.

For example:
1st set: 12 reps (50% 1RM)
2nd set: 10 repetitions (increasing kg)
3rd set: 8 repetitions (increasing kg)
4th set: 6 repetitions (increasing kg)
5th set: 4 repetitions (increasing kg)
You may continue with other sets by reducing the load and increasing the reps
6th set: 10 repetitions (decreases the kg)
7th set: 12 repetitions (decreases the kg)

DESCENDING PYRAMIDALS

In this case, we start with a high weight and we perform a few repetitions and with each repetition, we remove the weight and increase the repetitions.

For example:

=== Woman and Fitness ===

1st set: 85% 1RM X 5 reps (or to muscle failure)
2nd set: 80% 1RM X 6 reps (or to muscle failure)
3rd set: 75% 1RM X 7 reps (or to muscle failure)
4th set: 70% 1RM X 9 reps (or to muscle failure)

BULGARIAN METHOD (heavy / light)

It consists of performing a set to exhaustion with a high load and a range of repetitions ranging from a minimum of four to a maximum of six; once concentric exhaustion is reached, the weight to be lifted will be unloaded by 20-30% and you will continue to push until muscular exhaustion.

It is important to minimize the dwell time between the two sets as if we were in theory carrying out a single set which includes unloading of the weight lifted.

The purpose of the first part of the sets, that is the heavy sets, is to recruit a large number of white fibers and try to bring them to exhaustion.

With the second part of the sets, the one carried out after unloading the weight, it will be possible to continue working the fibers not yet recruited, also leading to exhaustion.

For this purpose, the unloading of the weight from the tool is decisive, which must be such (from 20 to 30% of the initial load) as to allow the work to be continued for the necessary time, performing at least 6 to 8 repetitions, to exhaust the availability energy of the fibers involved.

REST PAUSE

With this technique, you perform a limited number of repetitions (6 or 8) with a high weight (90% 1RM).

Reached exhaustion, rest for 15-20 seconds and perform a repetition, another rest of 15-20 seconds and do another repetition, continuing for another three or more repetitions.

REPETITIONS 1 and 1/4

With this technique, one repetition is performed. At the end of the lifting phase, a second repetition is performed but not for the entire arc of the movement as usual but a partial arc (usually a quarter of the movement), repeating the procedure for the number of repetitions provided.

It is therefore a question of stopping in the final position of the movement and going back by ¼ of the movement and performing the partial repetition.

FORCED REPETITIONS

This is a method that involves the help of a training partner who, after muscle failure has been reached, helps to complete a certain number of other repetitions by lifting the weight.

21 (7 + 7 + 7)

This technique involves performing 21 consecutive repetitions for each set by dividing them into three different movements: 7 repetitions by lifting the load up to mid-movement, 7 repetitions with the full range of motion, and 7 repetitions from the intermediate to the final position of maximum contraction.

There may be different variations based on the moment in which the complete movement is performed, which can be performed at the beginning, in the middle, or at the end of the sets.

BULLDOZER SET

This method consists of completing a predetermined number of repetitions, usually from 30 to 50, stopping each time you reach muscle failure, and then resuming the sets until you reach the established number of repetitions. The longer the set goes on, the more rest must increase between one partial set and another.

INTERRUPTED SET

This method involves performing 5 repetitions with a weight equal to 80% 1RM and then rest for 20 seconds, perform another 5 repetitions with the same weight, rest another 20 seconds and perform other repetitions until failure. After a 3 minute break, do a new set.

SUPER SLOW

This method involves performing the repetitions in the slowest and most controlled way possible, for both the eccentric and concentric phases, for example, 10 seconds for the concentric phase and 5 seconds for the eccentric phase.

STRIPPING

With this technique, a certain number of repetitions are performed with a high load and the weight is gradually decreased by performing the maximum possible number of repetitions at each load change. For example, we start with 80% 1RM for 5-6 repetitions, unload the weight (10-15%), and when muscle exhaustion is reached, unload again and do repetitions until muscle exhaustion.

SUPERSET

It involves performing two exercises one after another, performing a set of one and a set of the other, and resting only at the end of the two sets. These are the main variants:

Superset for antagonist muscles. In this variant, the two exercises to be performed in superset refer to two antagonistic muscle groups, for example, Pectoral – Back or Biceps – Triceps or Quadriceps – Femoral.

Superset for same muscle group: The two exercises to be performed in superset refer to the same muscle group.

Usually, the superset consists of a basic multi-joint exercise and a secondary one which is usually an isolation exercise. A classic example would be for pectoral muscles: Barbell flat bench pushes + Dumbbell incline bench pushes. Or for the lats: Lat-machine tractions + Pulley.

TRISET

A technique similar to supersets, but the exercises to be performed are three, usually of the same muscle group. It allows great muscular exhaustion. This technique is usually used on large muscle groups that can support these types of work such as the pecs, lats, quadriceps.

=== Andrea Raimondi ===

=== Woman and Fitness ===

Periodization

Periodizing means planning a training program by managing the training variables to ensure optimal response from the body concerning the goal you want to achieve.

Based on the theory of general adaptation syndrome, it is assumed that the body subjected to the stress of exercise reacts by increasing protein synthesis and other metabolic mechanisms that lead to the overcompensation of the proteins of the muscles, thus initiating the process of increase and strengthening of the capabilities of the muscles themselves.

But over time the muscle, if subjected to the same stimulus, slows down or stops growth precisely due to the body's ability to adapt. Hence the need to vary the training stimuli by altering the training variables to ensure the desired compensatory response.

Periodizing also means inserting the single training session within a cycle of sessions.

Usually, we speak of the **macrocycle**, **mesocycle**, and **microcycle**.

The microcycle can be considered a single week of sessions, the mesocycle groups a set of microcycles and a set of mesocycles constitutes the macrocycle.

The art of bodybuilding and body recomposition essentially consists of planning (and executing!) Micro, Meso, and macrocycles are functional to the acquisition of muscle mass, obviously without forgetting the role of proper nutrition.

[99]

It is clear that the optimal solution consists in finding the training plan tailored to each individuality: correct planning will prevent the body from getting practiced to the training stress, as we said because we can make changes in training variables: intensity, volume, rest intervals, frequency, exercise selection, the effort required.

Hence the need to periodize muscle stimuli.

Three types of periodization can be identified: **traditional** or linear periodization, **non-linear** or wavy periodization, and **inverse** periodization. In traditional periodization, there is an inverse relationship between volume and intensity, alternating mesocycles with high volumes and low intensity to mesocycles with low volumes and high intensity (load).

So we pass from a period of high volumes to one of the low volumes by increasing the intensity. This can lead to an increase in metabolic stress and lead in some cases (but this ultimately applies to the high-level athlete) to the threshold of overtraining. To overcome the problems of metabolic stress induced by traditional periodization and to maintain a greater hypertrophic state (the volume, as we know, is one of the factors of hypertrophy), several changes have been proposed to the traditional approach. Some of these approaches propose varying volume and intensity within the same mesocycle, alternating high-volume weeks with high-intensity weeks. The inverse periodization leads to the insertion of a period of hypertrophy, i.e. increasing the volume and reducing the load, at the end of a macrocycle.

At present, however, there is no scientific evidence on which is the best approach for hypertrophy, as it ultimately depends on the individual response to the set of factors that govern hypertrophy, i.e. it will never be possible to reproduce the same conditions on one person who uses the traditional periodization approach first and then the wave periodization approach.

Ultimately, the individual response given by one's genetics counts, all other conditions being equal. How many muscle fibers of type I and type II an individual have in his muscles. Someone will get more muscle development from high volume and low intensity, others from high intensity and low volume.

The magic and skill of the trainer consist in using and manipulating the training variables to find the best solution for the individual, ensuring a condition that does not reach overtraining.

In general, we can for convenience keep in mind the following values to create our workout plans.

Metabolic phase
sets: 2/3
Reps: 20/25
Load up to 60% 1RM

Hypertrophy phase
sets: 3/4
Reps: 6/12
Load at 60% -80% 1RM

Strength phase

setss: 4/5

Reps: 3/5

Load at 85% -100% 1RM

We can build on these parameters the periodization of the meso-cycle or microcycle by varying volume and weight. We can also decide, inside the mesocycle, to adopt full-body strategies or strategies based on split routines. With full-body training, all the main muscle groups are trained in each session, with split routines only certain areas are trained in each session (upper body / lower body or a mix of the two). The choice depends on the time available and the individual's training skills.

Full Body example

at each session

Bench press

Pulley or lat machine

Curl

Pull down

Squat or leg press

leg curl

calf

crunch

High / low split example

alternating between sessions

day A

Bench press

Pulley or lat machine

Curl

=== **Woman and Fitness** ===

Pull down
day B
Squat or leg press
leg curl
calf
crunch

An example of **traditional periodization** consist of the following mesocycles:
4 weeks full-body general conditioning with three sessions per week
4 weeks full body hypertrophy with three sessions per week
4 weeks full-body strength with three sessions per week
An example of **wavy periodization** can be the following:
3 weeks full-body general conditioning with three sessions per week
1 week full body hypertrophy with three sessions per week
1 week full-body strength with three sessions per week
1 week full body general conditioning with three sessions per week
1 week full body hypertrophy with three sessions per week
1 week full-body strength with three sessions per week
or
3 weeks general conditioning with split routine on four days a week
2 week hypertrophy with split routine on four days a week
2 week strength with split routines on four days a week

[103]

1 week general conditioning with split routine on four days a week
2 week hypertrophy with split routine on four days a week
2 week strength with split routines on four days a week
or again we can use split routines in the microcycle by dividing the week into days of hypertrophy and days of strength and after 4-6 weeks introduce a week of rest.

As you can see, keeping in mind the fixed points discussed above, we can create infinite combinations in microcycles and mesocycles based on the individual response.

In this regard, it is necessary to keep track of the trends of the various sessions and then note the work done in terms of sets, repetitions, and weight used as well as the recovery time. To better understand how the body responds to training, it is also necessary to take note of some parameters such as weight, temperature, circumferences, heart rate.

=== Woman and Fitness ===

Major Muscle Groups

We review in this chapter the main muscle groups of the human body.

Muscles of the back
Chest muscles
Muscles of the abdomen
Shoulder muscles
Muscles of the arms
Leg muscles

The best exercises with *free weights* and *machines* will be illustrated for each of them.

The difference between the types of exercises is quite evident.

Bodyweight exercises use the weight of your body as a load. Free weight exercises use tools such as barbells and dumbbells. Exercises with machines use the classic equipment that we find in the gym.

The main difference between exercises with free weights and with machines consists in that with the first the movements do not have a fixed execution trajectory, which instead occurs using machines. Which requires a more precise movement if we want it and which is more concentrated on the target muscle.

Certainly with each of these types you can get results. These always depend on this respect, for example with free-body, we will look for a progression in the number of sets and repetitions, not

[105]

being able to increase your body weight between one set and another.

This principle of progression is also valid for the other types of exercises, to which we can add in these cases the variable of the load to be used also. So in addition to increasing (or decreasing) the number of sets and repetitions, we can increase (or decrease) the weights lifted.

Which one is better? This is a useless question.

Everyone can have their preferences for one exercise or another but given the need to vary the type of exercises and to hit the muscle differently, to avoid as much as possible the adaptation of the body to the stimuli to which it is subjected, it is good to use, when possible, a plurality of types of exercise. What I want to emphasize here is the fact that even with the few tools available you can improve your body. So there are no excuses: even in times of lockdown or without gyms we must not give up and always strive towards the goal of improving our fitness.

Of course, always with knowledge and following a given progression: it makes no sense to vary your training routine every week. However, between one mesocycle and the next, it is good to vary, for example, the type of exercise and the individual exercises that affect a certain muscle district.

The exercises and their variations from this point of view are almost infinite.

In any case, it is good to remember that the muscles and joints to which the first are connected are always the same. It is better to identify some exercises or their variants without necessarily

=== Woman and Fitness ===

looking for novelty, but rather, as mentioned, try to ensure a progression of training stimuli in one's routine.

With this in mind, it is essential for those who want to train, to know the motor patterns of the joints whose muscles act as motors.

Muscles of the Back

The back muscles are the muscles located in the posterior region of the trunk, in the area between the neck and buttocks. They can be divided into two sub-categories, which have different functions and characteristics: the deep and superficial muscles.

The deep layer of the back musculature is composed of the so-called erector spinae muscles, long muscle bundles that extend from the lower back to the cervical, including, among others, the multifidus, the iliocostal and the longissimus. These muscles, together with the interspinous and inter-transversal muscles, have the important function of extending the back, keeping it erect and stabilizing the vertebrae especially during the movements of the trunk and limbs. They are muscles not visible except in the lumbo-sacral area, where two cords of muscle tissue can be seen.

The superficial layer is instead composed of muscles such as the latissimus dorsi muscle, the largest muscle in the human body. It originates at the level of the pelvis, the thoracic-lumbar belt, the thoracic vertebrae and the ribs to insert at the level of the crest of the minor tubercle. It is a fundamental muscle in movements such as climbing, as it is an extensor, adductor and internal rotator of the shoulder, as well as an extensor of the trunk and an anteversion of the pelvis.

Always in the most superficial area of the back we have the rhomboid muscles divided into small and large, which are located in the center of the back and which move from the medial margin of the scapula to the lower cervical and upper thoracic vertebrae.

These muscles allow the shoulder to be brought closer to the spine and are also stimulated during the pulling, rowing and climbing movements as synergistic as the latissimus dorsi.

The trapezius, formed by three portions, one upper, one middle and one lower, which covers the upper part of the back with an origin at the level of the nape, cervical and thoracic vertebrae, to insert on the shoulder blade and collarbone. It extends the cervical and allows the scapula to be moved with elevation and cranial rotation (superior), adduction (middle) and depression (inferior).

The quadratus lumborum muscle, on the other hand, is a small muscle located from the pelvis to the last rib and the lumbar vertebrae, which allows you to extend and tilt the spine.

Exercises for the back muscles

All exercises such as tractions, pull downs and lat machines that reproduce the movement of climbing and all pulling exercises such as pulley, rowing and body row.

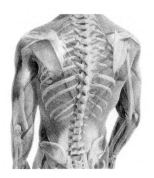

=== Andrea Raimondi ===

=== Woman and Fitness ===

Chest Muscles

In this area, the main muscles are the pectoralis major and the pectoralis minor

The pectoralis major originates with its muscle bundles at the level of the anterior border of the clavicle with its clavicular portion, at the level of the sternal bundle, and costal cartilages with its sternocostal portion and at the level of the rectus sheath with its abdominal portion.

All the fibers converge to anchor with a cross insertion on the crest of the greater tubercle of the humerus. The muscular belly of the pectoralis major entirely covers the pectoralis minor, placed under it.

These muscles have the function of adduction, flexion thanks to the claveal bundles, extension from the position of maximum flexion mainly using the sternocostal and abdominal bundles, and internal rotation of the humerus.

Adduction: movement that brings a limb closer to the midline of the body

Flexion: movement that tends to bring two segments of the body or a limb closer together

Abduction: to draw or spread away (a part of the body, such as a limb) from a position near or parallel to the median axis of the body or from the axis of a limb

Internal rotation: the rotational movement that the limb makes around its axis, towards the midline of the body

[111]

The pectoralis formed of three different portions: the clavicular one, the sternocostal one, and the abdominal one.
The different direction of the fibers of these three portions determines the anatomical functions of the pectoral muscles:
with the clavicular bundles: adducts, flexes the humerus;
with the sternocostal bundles: adducts the humerus;
with the abdominal bundles: adducts, and extends the humerus from the position of maximum flexion (starting with the arm above the head).

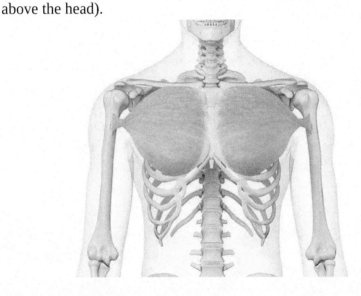

Pectoralis minor
Pectoralis minor originates on the third, fourth, and fifth ribs and is inserted at the level of the scapula, on the choroid process. It is therefore a muscle that allows the movements of the rib cage and

scapula. It is located immediately under the pectoralis major muscle, which covers it.

It allows for depression, caudal rotation, and an anterior tilt of the scapula. It acts as a secondary muscle in inspiration.

Examples of exercises to train and develop the chest are the flat bench with barbell or dumbbells, dumbbells cross, push-ups and the incline bench.

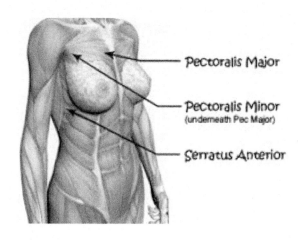

Abdominal Muscles

The muscle group of the abdominal area is composed of a set of different muscles that work in synergy and that are superimposed on each other: the rectus abdominis muscle, the most famous and the most superficial, which originates from the costal cartilages and the xiphoid process of the sternum and with an insertion at the level of the pubic crest of the pelvis, it has a vertical course with its fibers. It is not possible to recruit only the upper part or only the lower part through appropriate exercises or movements.

During flexion of the trunk, for example, by performing a classic crunch or a reverse crunch, the rectus abdominis always activates in its entirety;

The **transverse abdominal** muscle, the deepest, which with its origins at the level of the thoracolumbar fascia, inguinal ligament, iliac crest, and costal cartilages and with its insertion at the level of the lunate line and abdominal aponeurosis. The transverse has the fibers with a transversal course;

The **external oblique** muscle, more superficial, with its origins at the level of the 5-12 costal interval and with its insertions at the level of the iliac crest and abdominal aponeurosis, the external oblique has a vertical course with its fibers more external, which are inserted on the iliac crest, and oblique course with the fibers having insertion on the aponeurosis moving from top to bottom and from back to front; this muscle allows to reverse the pelvis, it flexes and tilts the trunk laterally, rotates the trunk.

The **internal oblique** muscle, deeper, with its origins from the iliac crest and the thoracolumbar fascia and its insertions at the level of the abdominal aponeurosis and the last three ribs, the internal oblique has an opposite trend to the external oblique muscle, from below up and from front to back.

This muscle compresses the viscera, flexes and rotates the trunk, tilts the trunk.

More generally, the first function of the whole of the abdominal muscles is the compression of the viscera, which, without adequate containment given by any bone structure, needs this specific muscular apparatus to be adequately supported.

The **rectus abdominis** is a muscle that flexes the spine and reverses (turns backward) the pelvis and is the protagonist in all the exercises generally proposed in the gym, Crunch above all, but also cross Crunches (which are erroneously referred to as exercises with a focus on oblique muscles), Reverse Crunches, Plank, AB Wheel and Sit-ups.

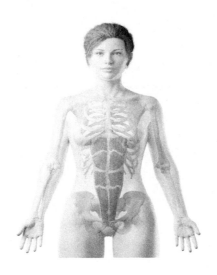

Shoulder Muscles

The main shoulder muscle to train is the deltoid which is usually divided into anterior, lateral, and posterior. It moves the joint complex of the shoulder.

The deltoid covers and protects the main joints of this anatomical district.

It abducts the shoulder, flexes and lets the internal rotation of the shoulder (anterior portion), extends, and lets the external rotation of the shoulder (posterior portion).

Main exercises are: lateral raises, front raises, rear raises, military press

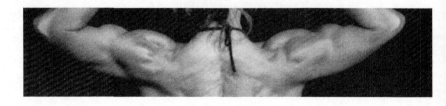

Arms Muscles

The arm muscles are located starting from the shoulder and from the humerus to the bones of the forearm, ulna, and radius.

The arm muscles move the scapulothoracic, scapulohumeral joint, and elbow.

We can distinguish shoulder flexor and elbow flexor muscles, located in front of the arm, and shoulder extensor and elbow extensor muscles, located behind the arm.

Between the flexor muscles of the elbow and shoulder, we have the biceps, made up of two distinct heads. The long head originates from the supraglenoid tubercle of the scapula. The short head originates from the choroid process of the scapula. The two distinct heads come together and are inserted with a common tendon at the level of the tuberosity of the radius. The brachial biceps as a whole are the most important flexor of the elbow but it is also a muscle that causes flexion of the shoulder and anterior tilt of the scapula (with its short head).

The main exercise for this muscle is the curl in its many variations.

The main muscle of the back of the arm is the brachial triceps, it is divided into three distinct heads. The long head originates at the level of the subglenoid tubercle of the scapula, the medial head, and the lateral head instead originate from the posterior aspect of the humerus respectively medially and laterally to the sulcus of the radial nerve. This muscle extends the shoulder and extends the elbow.

Arms Muscles Main exercises:
French press with barbell or dumbbell, Parallel dips, Push-ups with tight arms, Kick back with a dumbbell, Push down,

Muscles of the forearm

The brachioradialis, between the forearm muscles, participates in the flexion of the elbow.

The brachioradialis is a muscle that originates on the humerus and is inserted into the radius.

Exercises: Reverse grip curl, Wrist flexions with dumbbells, Wrist rotations with dumbbells.

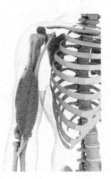

=== Woman and Fitness ===

Leg Muscles

We divide the muscles of the legs into anterior and posterior, between the muscles that are located in the front of the thigh. Certainly, the quadriceps femoris is the best-known muscle. It is made up of four different muscle bellies: the rectus femoris and the vastus, medialis, and lateralis.

The four heads are inserted with a common tendon at the level of the patella and through the patellar tendon to the tibia.

Its contraction allows you to extend the knee and flex the hip.

For these muscles, there are multiarticular or monoarticular exercises. The former activates the quadriceps through the simultaneous movement of multiple joints such as squats, lunges, step-ups, leg presses, among others. In this type of exercise, the quadriceps contract as a knee extensor together with muscles such as the gluteus maximus or the posterior hamstrings, which also extend the hip at the same time. Single-joint exercises, on the other hand, activate the quadriceps by moving only the knee joint, such as the leg extension.

In the rear part of the thigh are situated the hamstrings, among these, we find the hamstring muscle, the semitendinosus muscle, and the semimembranosus muscle. The hamstring muscles are so-called because they all originate from the ischium of the pelvis and are inserted in different points on the leg (crural).

This group of muscles allows you to extend the hip, reverse the pelvis and flex the knee. The hamstring rotates the knee externally, semitendinosus and semimembranosus rotate the knee internally. Among the exercises for this muscle group, we can mention Squats, deadlifts, lunges, step-ups, which are multi-joint, while the leg curl allows you to isolate the hamstring..

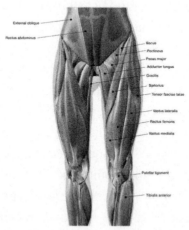

Calf. These muscles are anchored on the bones of the leg in numerous points including the distal femur, tibia, fibula, and foot bones and we can distinguish them in dorsiflexor muscles of the ankle, located anteriorly on the leg and plantar flexor muscles of the ankle, located posteriorly on the leg.

From our point of view, the main calf muscles we will deal with are located in the back of the leg and are the soleus muscle and the gastrocnemius muscle which together form the calf. The soleus is a muscle that originates posteriorly on the tibia and fibula. The gastrocnemius instead originates with two distinct heads (the twins) above the medial and lateral condyle of the femur. These two muscles join and enter through the Achilles tendon on the heel. They allow a plantarflexion movement of the ankle and allow supination and inversion of the foot also.

Among the exercises to train the calves, we remember the standing calf raise and their variants with machines or with free weights.

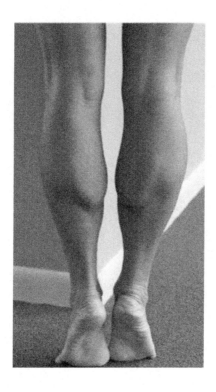

=== Andrea Raimondi ===

=== Woman and Fitness ===

PART II
Practice

=== Andrea Raimondi ===

=== Woman and Fitness ===

DIETING

=== Andrea Raimondi ===

=== Woman and Fitness ===

Food Diary

A food diary can be a simple sheet of paper on which you write everything you eat for at least 7 days, preferably for two weeks. Then all meals, snacks, or drinks you take are recorded.

Hiding information will prevent you from having an accurate picture of the calories consumed and therefore it will not be possible, later, to plan the meal plan correctly.

To have a valid overview, it is also essential to note the size of the portions of the individual meals (eg. 100 g of brown rice or 150 ml of orange juice).

Only in this way is it possible to determine exactly the amount of calories, including the ratio of the various nutrients.

The first few times it can be convenient to use a kitchen scale. Regarding the way information is represented in the food diary, there are no particular precautions. You can write the information in a table format or simply write it on paper or, again, on a tablet or laptop.

It is best to break down processed foods into ingredients. For example, instead of writing a "ham sandwich", write down the quantities of bread, ham, and toppings as separate entries.

The same goes for other cooked dishes. Not forgetting to also note the snacks.

It is advisable to take note of what you drink, including water, with the relative quantities.

Even if you do not have a kitchen scale, it is possible to evaluate the quantity consumed by measuring the food using cups, bowls, or other containers that have a specific measure.

This will contribute to the accuracy of the food diary. Estimating "by eye" is not accurate, and generally leads to underestimating food and total calorie intake.

If you eat at a restaurant or buy food that you can hardly weigh, the quantities will be estimated.

Along with the doses, you can also write the calorie content. Looking, perhaps online, for the nutritional information of a specific food.

It is also good to indicate the day, time, and place where you eat. It is a procedure that helps to identify the behavioral patterns of nutrition. The time must be detailed, rather than generic, such as, for example, "afternoon aperitif" or "midnight snack".

You can enter notes that describe the mood you had at that moment, or what you were doing. But they are not fundamental.

However, you are free to write what you want. Some also take note of appetite levels before and after meals. Or physical symptoms following the intake of some particular food, such as dairy products or certain vegetables, especially if you are looking for some food intolerance.

=== **Woman and Fitness** ===

Based on what we have said, a food diary should include at least the following items:

Day, Time, Food, Amount in grams, Calories, Notes

To produce a table like the following

Day	Time	Food	Quantity gr.	Calories	Note
09/26	7:30	Milk	250	105	Very Hungry

Those who want to be more precise can note, for each food, the **nutritional values** in proteins, carbohydrates, and fats.

Day	Time	Food	Quantity gr.	Calories.	Protein gr.	Carbohy-drates gr.	Fat gr.	Note
09/26	7:30	Milk	250	105	8,5	12,5	2,5	Very Hungry

And we proceed the same way with all the food ingested.

Why we eat too much?

The food sector is an economic sector that, like any other in this kind of society, must continually expand its market to guarantee an average profit adequate to maintain the investments made in the sector itself. This is why we are continually exposed to food advertisements, television programs about food, which transform food itself into entertainment, into something that ultimately uses food for something other than its main purpose. The main purpose of food is to introduce energy sources and elements into the body to build and maintain tissue structures efficiently.

The frequent use of snacks and abuse of appetizing and high-fat foods, often ignoring the stimuli of hunger and satiety, express the search for gratification and fulfillment. Induced by advertising or motivations more psychological than physiological necessity. Obese people are more satisfied with foods rich in fat and with a high-calorie density and, therefore, are inclined to consume foods of this type. Meals rich in fatty foods produce a less intense and prolonged sense of satiety than that produced by foods rich in proteins and complex carbohydrates, even if the amount of calories is the same. This ensures that the tasty and high-calorie snack is consumed even in the absence of a hunger stimulus. Furthermore, it is clear that to sell any product, it must be made as attractive as possible. Foods with a high energy density are, in most cases, even the most palatable. The palatability, in turn, triggers mechanisms of pleasure and satisfaction in the body, which create a vicious circle that pushes people to eat more and more.

=== Woman and Fitness ===

Tips for not overeating

The first tip is to not skip main meals, to avoid eating continuously between meals. Whenever you feel the stimulus of hunger, outside the time set for the meal, you have to find a way to devote yourself to an activity that distracts you for the time necessary for that stimulus to pass: just resist 3 - 5 minutes. Or drink water. Avoid shopping when you are too hungry, and focus, once at the supermarket, on what we have indicated in the shopping list, without being distracted by what the supermarket offers.

Do not buy food that is not part of the diet or that we want to eliminate from our eating habits: the less food you have available during any hunger pangs, the easier it is to keep on the path of the diet to follow. However, keep a good supply of fruit and vegetables available, to replace junk foods or snacks, or aperitifs. Replace spirits with water, even sparkling water.

Meal Plan

In this chapter, we will highlight some procedures for the construction of a meal plan that can guarantee the correct intake of macronutrients and that is aimed to achieve the goals of weight loss and muscle mass.

In all cases, it is essential to determine a starting point.

The starting point is given by the calculation for one's TDEE, that is the value in kilocalories of one's energy needs. This level of kilocalories represents the pivot on which the whole food strategy is based. We know that it defines the amount of energy necessary to guarantee a state of equilibrium, which derives from the energy consumption given by one's physical constitution and one's level of activity.

Once we have obtained the TDEE, we know that, if we want to reduce fat mass, we must introduce some kilocalories lower than that level; if, on the other hand, you want to increase muscle mass, you must increase the number of kilocalories to exceed the TDEE, through an adequate plan and which necessarily involves adequate physical exercise. Deciding to increase calorie intake without a corresponding training plan leads, over time, only to increase the level of fat mass. It must always be remembered that weight loss is never localized only in a given area of the body, such as the abdomen, hips, arms, but occurs overall. Which areas of the body are first involved in the weight loss process depends on one's genetic makeup and varies from individual to individual. We have seen how, on average, for women, fat is deposited in preference on the hips and thighs. Exercise in the weight loss process serves to increase calorie consumption and increase lean mass, made up of muscles, ultimately allowing for better overall metabolism.

The TDEE is the ideal theoretical consumption and the ideal caloric intake.

At this point, it is necessary to know the actual weekly calorie consumption and, from this, to obtain a daily average. Through the food diary, kept for one or two weeks, we get precisely the amount of calories we have consumed in a given period. For this purpose, as already mentioned, it is essential to record all the foods consumed, with the relative quantities in grams and the relative calories. Even better if we also record the amount divided by macronutrients, carbohydrates, proteins, and fats, to get a more precise idea of our consumption. Once the two values relating to energy consumption have been obtained, the first step is to reach the caloric level defined by the TDEE. We have three possible scenarios given by the deviation of the actual income to TDEE: the deviation can be in excess, in deficit, or balance.

Based on the difference, we must think of a "meal plan" that permits us to reach, in its first phase, the value given by the TDEE, through some strategies that will be illustrated in the chapter dedicated to body recomposition.

The meal plan aims to define, for a given period of time, the appropriate quantities of macronutrients that allow to reach the daily kilocalories defined through the strategies to reach the TDEE. If, for example, we know that we must reach 1,600 kcal / day and we start from a consumption of 1,200 kcal / day, we must define in how many weeks we expect to reach the 1,600 kcal of the TDEE. If we decide for a gradual approach, we can decide to increase by 100 kcal every week. Then we will start by setting up a meal plan that provides us with 1,300 kcal / day the first week, 1,400 kcal / day the second week and 1,500 kcal / day the third week, up to the TDEE of 1,600 kcal / day, in our example, the fourth week. We will then proceed to a period of maintenance of a few weeks of the level reached. If, on the other hand, we are in an initial situation of excessive caloric consumption compared to the TDEE, we will proceed by decreasing the calories introduced weekly. In this case, for example, if we start with 2,000 kca / day, and we decide to decrease the consumption by 100 kcal per week, we will have: 1,900 kcal / day in the first week, 1,800 kcal / day the second, 1,700 kcal / day the third, until reaching the TDEE in the fourth week.

We can also think in terms of weekly calorie consumption. In this way, knowing what the weekly income should be, we can vary the daily intake, knowing that, if one day we ingest more calories, the following day or days, we will be able to eat less. Assuming a 1,600 kcal meal plan, we deduce that in a week we will have to eat foods that provide 11,200 kcal (1,600 x 7 days). To reach this quota we can also set up a diet that allows us to have one or two days with a caloric intake higher than 1,600 kcal on average: on Sunday, for example, we eat for 2,000 kcal., Offset by Tuesday and Thursday at 1,400 kcal, for recover the 400 kcal more than on Sunday. The effects of a given diet can be seen over time, by monitoring, through the indices and basic

=== Woman and Fitness ===

measures, which we indicate in the chapter dedicated to them, we will be able to follow our path and modify it in the case of results that are not adequate to what is expected.

The meal plan must provide for keeping the calories introduced through proteins and fats in place. For example, considering an intake of 1.5 grams of protein per kg of weight and 0.8 grams of fat per kg of weight, with a weight of 60 kg, we get the following values: 60 kg x 1.5 g. = 90 grams of protein, which corresponds to (90 g. X 4 kcal / g) 360 kcal, and 60 kg x 0.8 g. = 48 grams of fat which correspond to (48 g. X 9 kcal / g) 432 kcal.

In this case, by adding proteins and fats, we obtain 792 kcal, the rest will be obtained from carbohydrates and, that is, referring to the TDEE of our example, 1,600 - 792 = 808 kcal, which correspond to (808/4 kcal / g) 202 grams of carbohydrates per day. In this example we have the following percentages among the macronutrients:

carbohydrates 50%

protein 23%

fats 27%

By keeping the levels of proteins and fats steady, it is evident that the changes, increasing or decreasing, depending on the case, are dependent on the level of carbohydrates. By increasing them in the event of an initial deficit compared to the TDEE or decreasing them in the event of a caloric surplus compared to the TDEE.

=== Andrea Raimondi ===

=== Woman and Fitness ===

Meal Plan in Practice

Let's see in practice how to calculate the number of macroelements and the relative kcal, to set up a meal plan. For this, we take for example a typical day in which our high-calorie diet expects to consume about 1,600 kcal.

You will find the details of this diet in the next chapter.

The number of kcal must be searched for each food chosen. These are usually defined as the amount of 100 g. or 100 ml of a given food. On this basis, the kcal relating to the quantity to be used will be calculated. Many apps make it easier to find the quantities of macronutrients and relative kcal for each food.

Let's start with breakfast. The diet includes the consumption of 250 ml of semi-skimmed milk and 70 grams of biscuits. 100 ml of semi-skimmed milk contains 4.8 grams of carbohydrates, 3.3 grams of protein, and 0.9 grams of fat, for a total of about 40 kcal. In our case, we have to multiply these values by 2.5 because we eat 250ml. So we will have 12 grams of carbohydrates, 8.25 grams of protein, and 2.25 grams of fat, for a total of 100 kcal. We do the same procedure for the other food provided, dry biscuits. In this case, the diet expects the consumption of 70 grams. We will therefore have to multiply the nutritional values of the reference 100 grams by 0.7 (70 grams / 100 grams). For convenience, I have reported the data in the table below. The same operation must be repeated for all the foods that make up the diet.

[137]

Modify the quantities to be consumed until you reach the calories provide by the plan.

Breakfast

Food	Kcal per 100 ml/gr	Kcal of example	Carbohydrates per 100 ml/gr	Carbohydrates of example	Protein per 100 ml/gr	Protein of example	Fat per 100 ml/gr	Fat of example
Low-fat milk ml 250	40	100	4,8	12	3,3	8,25	0,9	2,25
Biscuits gr 70	446	312	74	51,8	6,9	4,83	13,8	9,7
Totali		412		63,8		13,18		11,95

Lunch

Food	Kcal per 100 ml/gr	Kcal of example	Carbohydrates per 100 ml/gr	Carbohydrates of example	Protein per 100 ml/gr	Protein of example	Fat per 100 ml/gr	Fat of example
Mozzarella g. 100	254	254	2,8	2,8	24,2	24,2	15,9	15,9
Tomatoes gr. 200	20	40	3,5	7	0,8	1,6	0,2	0,4
Olive oil gr.10	884	88,4	0	0	0	0	100	10
Bread gr. 80	271	217	50	40	8,8	7	3,5	2,8
Total		599,4		49,8		32,8		29

=== Woman and Fitness ===

Dinner

Food	Kcal per 100 ml/gr	Kcal of example	Carbohydrates per 100 ml/gr	Carbohydrates of example	Protein per 100 ml/gr	Protein of example	Fat per 100 ml/gr	Fat of example
Rice gr. 100	358	286	79	63	6,5	5	0,5	0,4
Tomato puree gr. 30	38	11,4	9	2,7	1,65	0,5	0,21	0,06
Olive oil gr.5	884	44,2	0	0	0	0	100	5
Fillet of Beef gr.100	140	140	0	0	21,6	21,6	5,5	5,5
Beetroot gr 200	43	86	9,6	19,2	1,6	3,2	0,2	0,4
Cherries gr. 100	63	63	16	16	1	1	0,2	0,2
Totali		630,6		100,9		31,3		11,56

[139]

On the following pages, I have indicated a series of typical meal plans based on a certain caloric level. For the first "diet" I reported, which is 1,400 kcal, find a complete week. Based on the caloric level suited to your situation and your goal, you can modify the quantities of the various foods, adding or removing the necessary quantities until you reach the required caloric level.

1,400 kcal diet. A typical week.

Monday	
Breakfast	200 gr of semi-skimmed milk, 30 gr of wholemeal rusks, 30 gr of light jam
Snack	150 gr of fresh fruit
Lunch	vegetables to taste, 100 gr of mozzarella, 30 gr of rice cakes, 15 gr of olive oil
Snack	100 gr of fresh fruit
Dinner	vegetables to taste, 100 gr of grilled turkey breast, 15 gr of biscuits

=== Woman and Fitness ===

1,400 kcal diet.

Tuesday	
Breakfast	200 gr of semi-skimmed milk, 30 gr of wholemeal rusks, 30 gr of light jam
Snack	150 gr of fresh fruit
Lunch	vegetables to taste, 60 gr of rice or spelled, 15 gr of olive oil, 100 gr of peeled shrimp
Snack	100 gr of fresh fruit
Dinner	vegetables to taste, 120 gr of steamed salmon, 10 gr of olive oil, 15 gr of rice cakes

1,400 kcal diet..

Wednesday	
Breakfast	200 gr of semi-skimmed milk, 30 gr of wholemeal rusks, 30 gr of light jam
Snack	150 gr of fresh fruit
Lunch	salad to taste, tomatoes to taste, 100 gr of feta cheese, 15 gr of extra virgin olive oil, 30 gr of wholemeal bread
Snack	100 gr of fresh fruit
Dinner	120 gr of baked chicken breast, 15 gr of rice cakes, 10 gr of olive oil

=== Woman and Fitness ===

1,400 kcal diet.

Thursday	
Breakfast	200 gr of semi-skimmed milk, 30 gr of wholemeal rusks, 30 gr of light jam
Snack	150 gr of fresh fruit
Lunch	vegetables to taste, 60 gr of semolina, 100 gr of natural tuna, 30 gr of wholemeal bread, 15 gr of olive oil
Snack	100 gr of fresh fruit
Dinner	dried lentils 40 gr, vegetables to taste, 10 gr of rice cakes, 10 gr of extra virgin olive oil

1,400 kcal diet.

Friday	
Breakfast	200 gr of semi-skimmed milk, 30 gr of wholemeal rusks, 30 gr of light jam
Snack	150 gr of fresh fruit
Lunch	120 grams of drained canned chickpeas, vegetables to taste, 20 gr of extra virgin olive oil, 30 gr of wholemeal bread
Snack	100 gr of fresh fruit
Dinner	200 gr of sole, 15 gr of crackers, 10 gr of olive oil, vegetables to taste

=== Woman and Fitness ===

1,400 kcal diet.

Saturday	
Breakfast	200 gr of semi-skimmed milk, 30 gr of wholemeal rusks, 30 gr of light jam
Snack	150 gr of fresh fruit
Lunch	150 gr of baked chicken breast, vegetables to taste, 15 gr of biscuits, 10 gr of extra virgin olive oil
Snack	100 gr of fresh fruit
Dinner	Pizza margherita, vegetables to taste

1,200 kcal diet, with the following nutritional values:

NUTRIENTS	QUANTITY	ENERGY %
Proteins	50 g	18
Fat	36 g	26
Carbohydrates	176 g	56

Breakfast	Grapefruit juice 300 g Rusks 30 g Jam (such as living fruit) 15 g
Snack	Semi-skimmed milk yogurt 250 g
Lunch	Rye bread 70 g Canned beans 150 g Olive oil 10 g Tomato preserves 50 g Kiwi 100 g
Snack	Apple 200 g
Dinner	Durum wheat bread 40 g Garlic + capers 10 g Grilled aubergines 100 g Mozzarella 80 g

=== Woman and Fitness ===

1,600 kcal diet, with the following nutritional values:

NUTRIENTS	QUANTITY	ENERGY %
Proteins	81 g	20
Fat	63 g	36
Carbohydrates	187 g	44

Breakfast	Partially skimmed milk 300 g Rusks 40 g Jam 30 g
Snack	Semi-skimmed milk yogurt 130 g Apricots 150 g
Lunch	Pumpkin tortellini 120 g Grated Parmesan 10 g Rabbit, grilled lean meat 100 g Olive oil 10 g Spinach 200 g
Snack	Wholemeal biscuits 50 g Hazelnuts 10 g
Dinner	Durum wheat bread 80 g Tomato and basil 50 g Canned beans 100 g Olive oil 10 g

1,800 kcal diet, with the following nutritional values:

NUTRIENTS	QUANTITY	ENERGY %
Proteins	81 g	18
Fat	58 g	29
Carbohydrates	260 g	54

Breakfast	Partially skimmed milk 300 g Rusks 50 g Jam 30 g
Snack	Salty crackers 30 g Apple 200 g
Lunch	Brown rice 100 g Canned beans 200 g Butter 10 g Tomato preserves 30 g
Snack	Kiwi 100 g Dried walnuts 20 g
Dinner	Pork rump 150 g Green beans 200 g Extra virgin olive oil 10 g Durum wheat bread 50 g

=== **Woman and Fitness** ===

Dieta da 2.000 kcal circa, con i seguenti valori nutrizionali:

NUTRIENTS	QUANTITY	ENERGY %
Proteins	86 g	19
Fat	65 g	31
Carbohydrates	247 g	50

Breakfast	Orange juice 300 g Wafer biscuits 50 g
Snack	Semi-skimmed milk yogurt 130 g Muescli 20 g
Lunch	Semolina pasta 120 g Grated Parmesan 50 g Spinach 250 g Extra virgin olive oil 10 g
Snack	Apple 200 g Breadsticks 30 g
Dinner	Carrots 200 g Extra virgin olive oil 10 g Veal meat 150 g

[149]

Below, a series of examples of **high-calorie diets**, from which to take inspiration to build your food plan.

2,400 kcal diet, with the following nutritional values:

NUTRIENTS	QUANTITY	ENERGY %
Proteins	126 g	21
Fat	68 g	25
Carbohydrates	342 g	54

Breakfast	Orange juice 300 g Bread 70 g Apricot jam 40 g
Snack	Semi-skimmed milk yogurt 130 g Pine nuts 15 g Kiwi 100 g
Lunch	Brown rice 150 g Canned beans 150 g Extra virgin olive oil 20 g Parmesan g 20 g Preserves tomato + flavorings 50 g
Snack	Whey protein 90% 30 g Banana (peeled) 80 g
Dinner	Wholemeal bread 120 g Rabbit, lean meat 200 g Cucumbers 200 g Olive oil 20 g Apple 200 g

=== **Woman and Fitness** ===

2,600 kcal diet, with the following nutritional values:

NUTRIENTS	QUANTITY	ENERGY %
Proteins	146 g	22
Fat	86 g	29
Carbohydrates	339 g	49

Breakfast	Partially skimmed cow's milk 300 g Muesli 50 g Hazelnuts 20 g
Snack	Strawberries 150 g Low-fat milk yogurt with fruit 250 g
Lunch	Generic semolina pasta 150 g Grated Parmesan cheese 20 g Salad tomatoes 200 g Yellow peppers 100 g Olive oil 10 g Anchovies in oil 20 g Natural tuna 110 g
Snack	Apple 200 g
Dinner	Wholemeal bread 100 g 2 whole chicken eggs 120 g Corn oil 10 g Kiwi 100 g
After Dinner	Whey protein (90%) 25 g Semi-skimmed milk 250 g

2,750 kcal diet, with the following nutritional values:

NUTRIENTS	QUANTITY	ENERGY %
Proteins	128 g	19
Fat	93 g	30
Carbohydrates	374 g	51

Breakfast	Cup of tea 500 g Wholemeal rusks 100 g Sour cherry jam 40 g
Snack	Kiwi 100 g Dried walnuts 20 g
Lunch	Whole wheat semolina pasta 120 g Lean ground beef 150 g Tomato, a drizzle of oil and basil 50 g Courgettes 200 g
Snack	Olive bread 120 g Bresaola 50 g Apple 200 g
Dinner	Bruschetta type bread 100 g Tomatoes 150 g Black olives 20 g Olive oil 20 g Cow's mozzarella 100 g

=== **Woman and Fitness** ===

3,300 kcal diet, with the following nutritional values:

NUTRIENTS	QUANTITY	ENERGY %
Proteins	165 g	20
Fat	100 g	27
Carbohydrates	466 g	53

Breakfast	Semi-skimmed milk 300ml, 150kcal Oats 30g, 116.7kcal Rusks 45g, 191.7kcal Jam, general 25g, 69.5 kcal
Snack	Low-fat cottage cheese 100g, 86kcal Rye bread 60g, 154.8kcal Oranges 200g, 126kcal
Lunch	Lentils, 100g, 353kcal Parmesan 10g, 39.2kcal Red radicchio 100g, 23kcal Rye bread 90g 232.2kcal Extra virgin olive oil 20g, 180kcal
Snack	natural tuna 100g, 128kcal Rye bread 90g, 232.2kcal Kiwi 200g, 122kcal
Dinner	Baked blue fish Blue fish, average 200g, 248kcal Zucchini 300g, 48kcal Rye bread 120g, 309.6kcal Extra virgin olive oil 20g, 180kcal

=== Andrea Raimondi ===

=== Woman and Fitness ===

TRAINING

=== Andrea Raimondi ===

=== Woman and Fitness ===

EXERCISES

Chest
Free weight
Bench Press
Execution: Lie down on a flat bench, grip the barbell with hands aperture corresponding to the width of the shoulders; lower the bar slowly until it touches the middle part of the chest; push the bar to full arms extension without lifting your shoulders off the bench. You can replace the barbell with dumbbells.

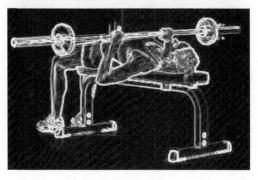

Incline bench press

Execution: Lie on a bench inclined at 45 or 60 degrees, grip the barbell with a grip corresponding to the width of the shoulders or the dumbbells; lower the bar or dumbbells slowly until it touches the upper chest; push the bar or dumbbells to full extension without lifting your shoulders off the bench.

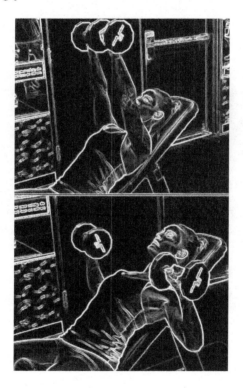

Dumbbell flyes
Execution: Lie down on a flat bench, hold two dumbbells with a neutral grip (with the palms of your hands facing each other); slowly lower the dumbbells while keeping the elbows locked to chest level; return to the starting position slowly still keeping the elbows locked.

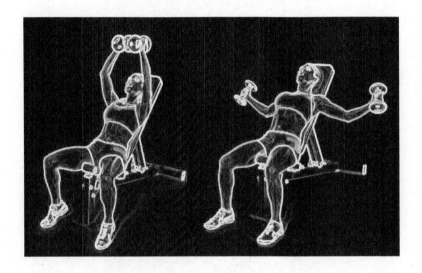

=== Woman and Fitness ===

Push-up
Execution: Lie on the ground with your arms slightly wider than your shoulders; lift your body without bending your back or knees. By increasing or decreasing arm distance you can work your triceps (tight grip) or shoulders (wide grip)

Parallel Bar Dips

Execution: Grasp the bars with shoulders blocked; bend the elbows until the forearms are parallel to the floor; return to the starting position.

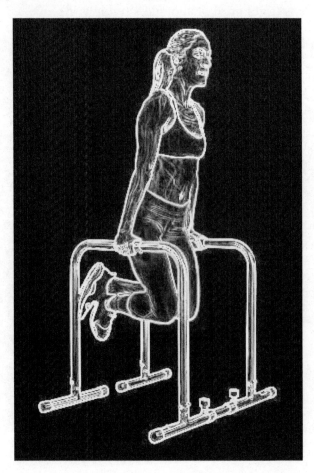

Bent arm pullover
Execution: Lying on a flat bench with the head on the edge move a dumbbell vertically; keeping the elbows partially bent, slowly lower the weight behind the head, while inhaling, until the weight reaches the height of the head; return exhaling to the starting position.

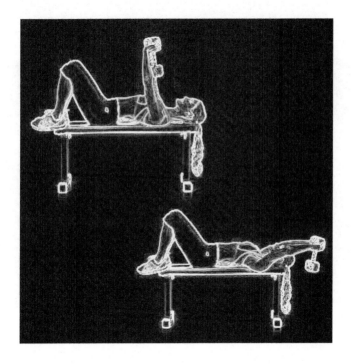

Machine
Chest press
Execution: Arrange the machine seat until your hands are at shoulder height. Push the bars slowly while exhaling; return to the starting position.

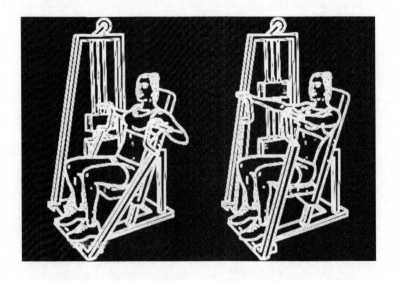

Pectoral Machine
Execution: Grasp the grips, move the bars slowly until the arms come together while exhaling; return to the starting position.

BACK
Free weight
Chin up
Execution: Grasp the bar with a prone grip at a width of about 15 cm greater than the shoulders; Raise the body until the chin touches the bar; lower the body slowly towards the starting position.

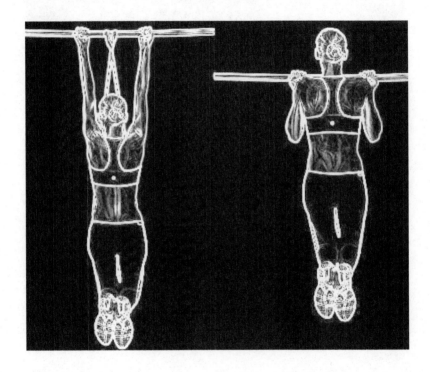

One arm dumbbell row

Execution: Hold a dumbbell with a neutral grip; Rest the opposite hand and knee on a bench; lift the dumbbell vertically by lifting the elbow as high as possible.

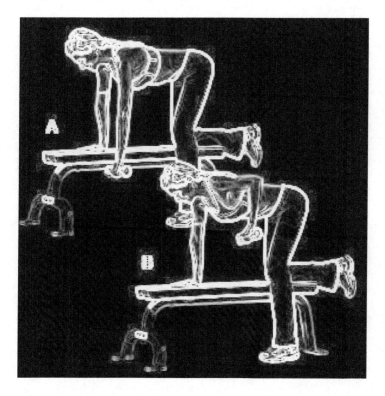

Dumbbell pull over

Execution: Lying on a flat surface with the head on the edge, support a handlebar vertically; keeping the elbows half-bent, slowly lower the weight behind the head while inhaling, until the weight reaches the height of the head; return exhaling to the starting position.

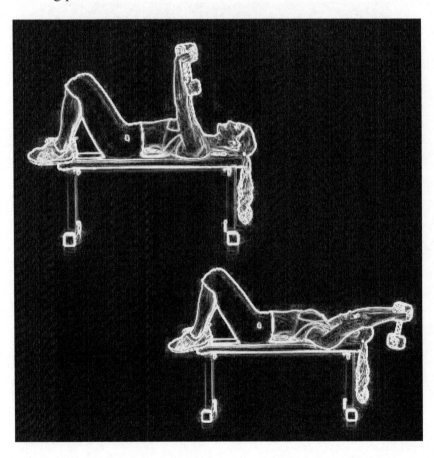

Machine
Lat machine o Cable front pull down
Execution: Grip the bar with a prone grip about 15 cm wider than that of the shoulders; Lower the bar until reaching the upper part of the chest, squeeze the back muscle; slowly return to the starting position.

Cable seated row
Execution: Sitting to the machine, grip the handle with a prone grip; pull the handle towards your chest while keeping your back straight; return to the starting position.

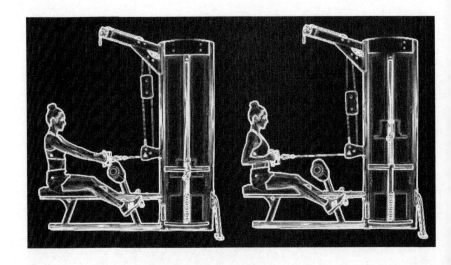

SHOULDERS
Free weight
Military press
Execution: Sitting on a bench, hold a barbell with a prone grip and with an opening slightly higher than the shoulders. Lower the bar until it reaches the chest in the collarbone area; slowly return to the starting position.

Distensioni con manubri o Seated dumbbell shoulder press
Execution: Sitting on a bench, two dumbbells are grasped at the sides of the head in pronation; rise to almost complete extension by approaching them slightly; slowly return to the starting position.

Dumbbell lateral raise

Execution: While standing, hold two dumbbells to the sides of the body. The arms are raised sideways and slowly until they reach shoulder height; slowly return to the starting position.

Dumbbell front raise

Execution: While standing, grasp two dumbbells holding them over the front of the thighs. The arms are raised frontally up to the height of the head. Slowly return to the starting position.

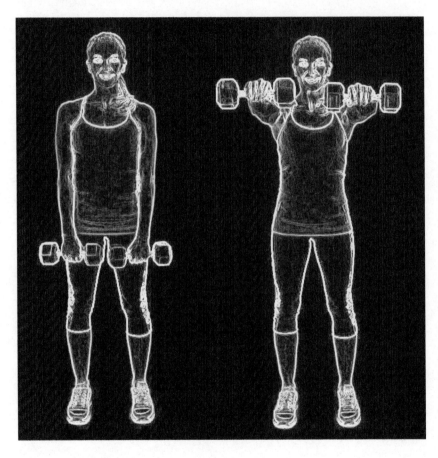

Rear lateral raises in piedi o Dumbbell rear lateral raise
Execution: Standing with the trunk almost in a horizontal position, hold two dumbbells keeping the elbows slightly bent; the dumbbells are raised laterally until they reach the height of the trunk; slowly return to the starting position.

Machine
Shoulder press
Execution: Sitting with the handles at shoulder height, the bars are pushed almost to the maximum extension of the elbow; slowly return to the starting position.

BICEPS

Free weight
Barbell curl
Execution: Standing, legs slightly apart, grip the barbell in front of the thighs; the barbell is raised slowly, keeping the shoulders still and moving only the elbow joint; return to the starting position.

Dumbbell curl
Execution: Standing with legs slightly apart or sitting on a bench, the dumbbells are held at the sides of the body with a neutral grip; the dumbbells are raised slowly, keeping the shoulders still and moving only the elbow joint; return to the starting position.

Machine
Cable curl
Execution: Standing in front of the low cable with the legs slightly apart, the bar is grasped in front of the trunk in supination (palms facing each other), with a handle slightly higher than the shoulders; raise the cable slowly keeping the shoulders still; return to the starting position.

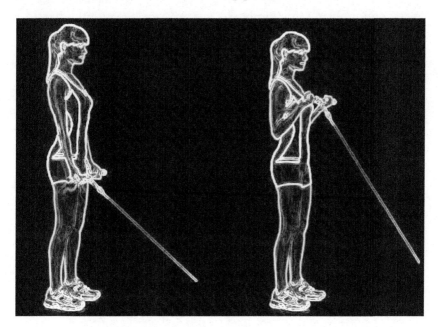

TRICEPS

Free weight
DB lying triceps extension
Execution: Lying on your back on a bench with your feet flat on the ground, grab the dumbbells with your hands in a neutral position with your elbows extended frontally in front of your eyes; slowly bring the dumbbells towards the sides of the head by bending the elbows; slowly return to the starting position.

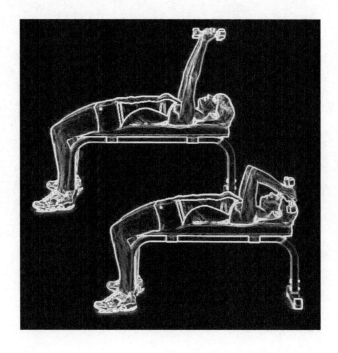

Bar dips

Execution: Holding the parallels with a tight grip lift yourself until your arms are fully extended, go down vertically slowly bending the elbows, until your arms are parallel to the floor; return to the starting position.

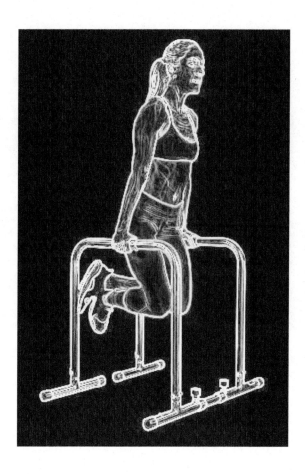

Dumbbell kick back

Execution: Holding a dumbbell in one hand, rest your free hand on a bench. Begin with the upper arm parallel to the floor and your elbow bent 90 degrees. Raise the dumbbell upward, straightening your arm until your elbow locks out.

Machine
Triceps Push down
Execution: Standing in front of the high cable, grasp the bar at a distance similar to or less than that of the shoulders; the bar is lowered without moving the elbows which are closed and close to the trunk; return to the starting position.

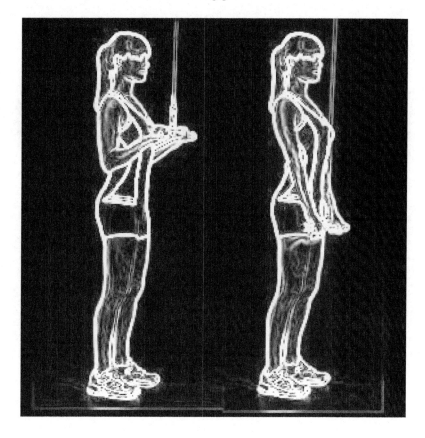

LEGS

Free weight
Dumbbell Squat
Execution: Standing with the legs slightly apart, holding a dumbbell in your hand; go down by bending the knees until the thighs are parallel to the ground, without raising the heels; return to the starting position.

Lunge

Execution: Standing with two dumbbells in the hand in a neutral position, take a long step forward, bringing the knee closer to the ground; return to the starting position.

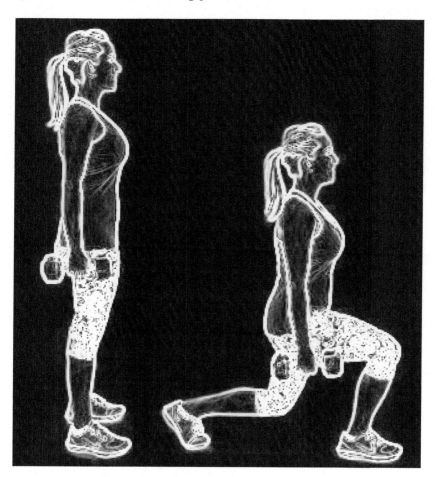

Hip Thrust

Execution: Lie down on a bench with your upper back. Take a dumbbell and hold it on your lap. Push the pelvis upwards, stop for 2 seconds in the position of maximum contraction of the buttocks.

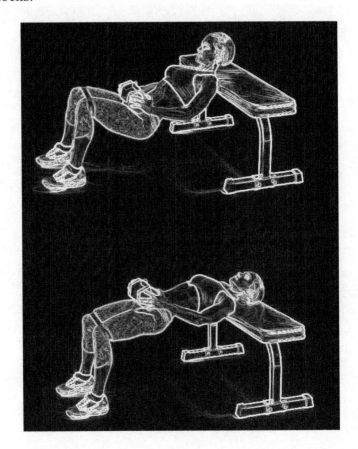

Step up

Execution: Stand in front of a rise or step, hold the dumbbells at your sides in a neutral position. Climb up and down the box, alternating legs.

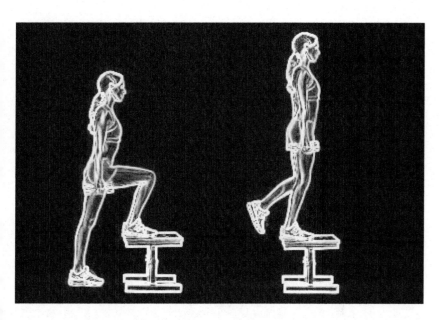

Standing calf raise

Execution: Standing with the front part of the foot resting on the edge of a step at a distance similar to the shoulders, perform a flexion of the sole of the foot; return to the starting position.

Macchinari

Machine
Leg press
Execution: Sitting at the machine with the back well supported, place the feet on the platform open slightly higher than that of the hips; go down until you bring the thighs closer to the trunk without raising the pelvis; return to the starting position.

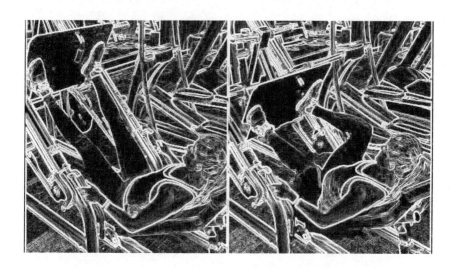

Leg extension

Execution: Sitting on the bench with the top of the ankles under the stops; raise the weight about 90 degrees until the legs are extended; slowly return to the starting position.

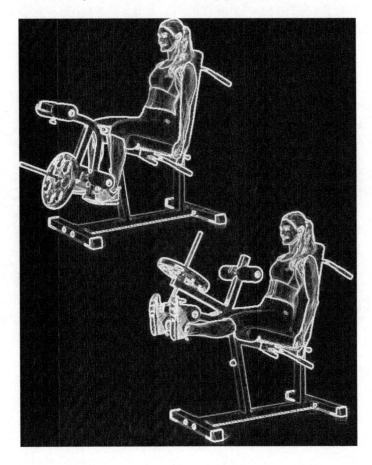

Leg curl
Execution: Lie down on the machine bench, place your heels under the machine stops and lift the weight; return to the starting position.

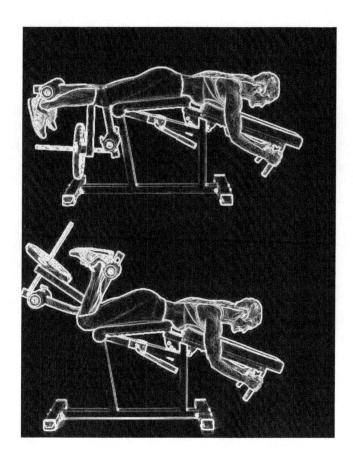

ABDOMINALS

Crunch
Execution: Lying on the back with the legs resting on a bench, the shoulders are raised with a contraction of the abdominals with a short and controlled movement, the lumbar area is always resting on the ground; return to the starting position.

Sit up

Execution: Sitting on a bench inclined of about 45 degrees with the legs under the supports, the trunk is raised with the contraction of the abdominals; return to the starting position.

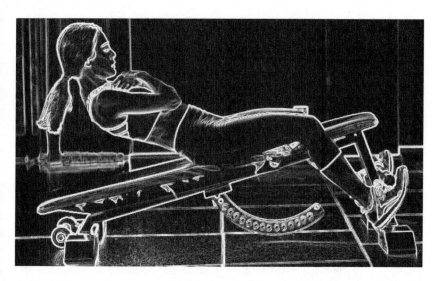

Lying leg vertical raise
Execution: Lying on the back with the hands on the sides of the body under the buttocks, raise the pelvis and bring the legs up with vertical movements, raising the lumbar area with each repetition; return to the starting position.

Some considerations

In my method, the time available for training is a fundamental component. For this, I propose to perform one or at most two exercises for each muscle group. Over time we "specialize" in the exercises chosen, gradually increasing the loads lifted.

Of course, if a muscle group does different joint functions, exercises must be alternated for each movement.

If we take the shoulder muscles, for example, we will perform a series of military presses and a series of lateral raises, or rear raises.

In general, I prefer only one exercise per muscle group, by the consideration that, in any case, all sectors of the muscle are involved in each movement performed.

Certainly, during the mesocycles, there will be variations in the type of exercise to ensure the necessary variability in this respect.

In any case, the type of exercise is the variable that has the least impact on muscle mass, if you can ensure the necessary increase in the main training variables. Which are, as we have seen, the load, the volume of training (sets and repetitions), and the duration of rest between sets.

My advice, in creating your training routines, is to train as many times as possible during the week, ensuring multi-frequency.

By training the same muscle district several times a week, with sessions of 30/40 minutes.

The training proposals that you will find in the next chapters are partly taken from my book "12 Months Workout". They fit both women and men. What can change is the amount of weight lifted, even though many women are stronger than many men. However, they are made to adapt to loads related to the capabilities of each person.

For those who are starting to train and perhaps want to lose weight, what matters is to activate the metabolism which in turn brings for improved insulin sensitivity and greater and better consumption of calories.

Muscle groups are the same for men and women and they all need to be trained. Of course, maybe some muscle areas that are weaker than others will be privileged. Each person is different, but you cannot think that women workouts should consist mainly of exercises for the thighs and buttocks.

=== Woman and Fitness ===

Aerobic activity

Aerobic activity is that type of motor activity that requires high consumption of oxygen as it lasts over time. As we have seen when talking about energy systems, the glycogen stores are depleted as a result of prolonged muscular work overtime; this leads to an increase in the use of energy reserves in the form of fats.

Aerobic activity is therefore useful in weight loss or in a phase of muscle definition, which can follow a so-called "mass" phase because it allows you to consume more calories than weight lifting. And obviously the longer the motor activity lasts over time, the higher the energy consumption will be. A moderate speed run is usually recommended, trying to keep your heart rate between 65 and 80% of your maximum heart rate.

This maximum heart rate can be obtained in a rough but indicative way with the following formula:

FCMax = 220 - age.

The minimum duration of aerobic activity recommended, to have a benefit over time in terms of physical condition and metabolic improvement, is at least 20 minutes per session.

In any case, you do not lose weight while doing the physical activity but maintaining a calorie deficit over time. Aerobic activity helps this process because it increases the consumption of calories and therefore allows the share of the aforementioned calorie deficit to be increased.

To get an idea of the role of aerobic activity in weight loss, we can use some useful formulas, developed over time by sports science scholars, such as the following:

Energy expenditure (Kcal) = 1Kcal x Kg of weight x Km traveled (Arcelli formula). For example 1Kcal x 60 (weight) x 10 (Km traveled) = 600 Kcal consumed.

Based on some studies, the percentages of use of carbohydrates and fats have been established as a function of the percentage of maximum heart rate, through the Respiratory Quotient and VO-max (oxygen consumption).

A heart rate below 80% of the maximum heart rate leads us to burn an average of 70% of carbohydrates and 30% of fat. Returning to our example, to know the amount of Kcal of fat burned we must calculate 30% of 600 Kcal, which corresponds to 180 Kcal. One gram of fat corresponds to 9 Kcal, but in the human body, the fat mass (adipocyte) is combined with water, for which 1Kg of body fat represents about 7,000 Kcal and not 9,000 Kcal, as it may seem by multiplying 1Kg by the 9 Kcal generated from a 1 gram of fat. So in practice, 1 gram of body fat corresponds to 7Kcal. In practice, in the training session of our example, 180 Kcal / 7 = 25.7 grams of fat were consumed. To lose, for example, 2.57 Kg. (25.7 grams * 1000 grams (1Kg)), keeping all other parameters unchanged, you have to travel 10,000 km. It is clear that to obtain results in terms of weight loss, one cannot ignore a diet that generates a long-term caloric deficit. And this is true regardless of the type of diet in vogue at any given time. You can also lose weight by eating

=== Woman and Fitness ===

more carbohydrates if your overall calorie intake is lower than your energy consumption.

Which aerobic activity to use? Much depends on personal preferences and the season. It is always preferable to carry out this activity outdoors, through running or jogging.

For those who start now with some aerobic activity, for example with running, I recommend starting with light activity, with 20-minute walks.

During the first phase, we will try to increase the duration of the training by 5-10 minutes at each outing, up to 45 minutes.

In the second phase, after the first 15 minutes of walking, a light run is started, to be held for 5 minutes. At this stage, we will try to increase the time in which we run each time, compared to the time in which we walk.

When you can run for at least 45 minutes, you can increase your running speed.

In this case, periods of slow running will alternate with periods of fast running.

For example, 15 minutes of slow running, 5 minutes of fast running, alternating between the two speeds during the training session, and trying each time to increase the duration of the fast run.

Phase 1 and phase 2 summary table for anaerobic training, in this case referring to running, of an untrained person. If you only practice aerobic activity, at least 3 workouts a week are recommended. If, on the other hand, you also practice weight training sessions, one or two sessions per week, depending on the type of

[199]

preparation (whether for strength, mass, or general conditioning).

	PHASE 1	Time in minutes	
	WALK TIME	RUNNING TIME	TOTAL TIME
WEEK 1	20		20
WEEK 2	30		30
WEEK 3	40		40
WEEK 4	45		45

	PHASE 2	Time in minutes	
	WALK TIME	RUNNING TIME	TOTAL TIME
WEEK 1	15	10	25
WEEK 2	15	15	30
WEEK 3	15	20	35
WEEK 4	15	25	40

Training Protocols

Below you will find the detail of my training protocol lasting a total of **32 weeks, 8 months of training**, at the end of which it is possible to continue, resuming a certain phase, **up to a year** of training.

This macrocycle is divided into *four phases*: an initial or **adaptation phase** lasting 8 weeks suitable for those who have just started training or for those who resume activity after a period of rest. This is followed by an 8 weeks **strength phase** in which we try to increase overall strength.

After the strength phase, very expensive for the body follows a **recovery phase** lasting 4 weeks.

The last mesocycle of the protocol consists of the **hypertrophy phase** lasting 12 weeks, in which the workouts will be aimed at gaining muscle mass.

At the end of the period of hypertrophy, it is good to insert a recovery period of another 4 weeks and then restart with a cycle of strength or with another cycle of hypertrophy based on your specific goals.

Adaptation phase (8 weeks)

This phase is designed for those who have never trained with weights or for those who have not trained for a long time.

Those who have been training for at least 6 months can use this phase as a preparation for the next ones or start directly with the strength phase.

The protocol provides for an 8-week mesocycle divided into two sections.

There are three days of training each week.

The first section has the main purpose of learning the movements of the various exercises. They train all major muscle groups in each training session.

They are "Full body" workouts in which the loads do not have to be heavy and the repetitions are quite high, from 15 to 20 per set, with rests of about 1 minute between sets.

It is important to start very gradually to allow the body to adapt to the effort without incurring injuries or annoying pains that can block your desire to train.

Always do one or two sets of warm-ups with a low load before each exercise.

Every week increase the maximum load used in the training series.

Phase two, also with full-body sessions and lasting four weeks, includes weeks with light loads and others with heavier loads.

Throughout the initial phase, but more generally during training, you must try to maintain a constant and **"clean" movement**, focusing on the muscle you are working on.

Keep an **execution speed** (TUT) of 2 seconds during the concentric phase and 2 seconds in the eccentric phase.

As for the **weight** to be lifted, this clearly varies according to your initial state of form and experience as well as your initial strength. To make the use of the cards universal, I have adopted the system relating to the maximum repetition, or rather the maximum number of repetitions that you can perform with a given weight. For example, if 3 series @ 8-10RM is indicated, it means that you must use a weight that allows you to perform a maximum of 10 repetitions correctly and not less than 8, if then in another card for the same exercise that number is lowered, for example, find @ 5-7RM means that with the weight used you can perform a maximum of 7 repetitions, i.e. the load is heavier than the first indication.

Adaptation phase. Section 1. Week 1
Perceived effort equal to 6

DAY	MUSCLES	EXERCICES
Monday	Full Body	Dumbbell bench press [3 sets @ 15-20RM] Dumbbell military press [3 sets @ 15-20RM] Dumbbell bent over row [3 sets @ 15-20RM] Dumbbell curl [3 sets @ 15-20RM] Cable pushdown [3 sets @ 15-20RM] Leg curl [3 sets @ 15-20RM] Squat [3 sets @ 15-20RM] Crunch [3 sets @ 15-20RM] Calf raise [3 sets @ 15-20RM]
Tuesday	Rest	
Wednesday	Full Body	Dumbbell bench press [3 sets @ 15-20RM] Dumbbell military press [3 sets @ 15-20RM] Dumbbell bent over row [3 serie @15-20RM] Dumbbell curl [3 sets @ 15-20RM] Cable pushdown [3 sets @ 15-20RM] Leg curl [3 sets @ 15-20RM] Squat [3 sets @ 15-20RM] Crunch [3 sets @ 15-20RM] Calf raise [3 sets @ 15-20RM]
Thursday	Rest	
Friday	Full Body	Dumbbell bench press [3 sets @ 15-20RM] Dumbbell military press [3 sets @ 15-20RM] Dumbbell bent over row [3 sets @ 15-20RM] Dumbbell curl [3 sets @ 15-20RM] Cable pushdown [3 sets @ 15-20RM] Leg curl [3 sets @ 15-20RM] Squat [3 sets @ 15-20RM] Crunch [3 sets @ 15-20RM] Calf raise [3 sets @ 15-20RM]
Saturday	Rest	Aerobic Activity
Sunday	Rest	

=== **Woman and Fitness** ===

Adaptation phase. Section 1. Week 2
Perceived effort level 7

DAY	MUSCLES	EXERCICES
Monday	Full Body	Dumbbell bench press [3 sets @ 15-20RM] Dumbbell military press [3 sets @ 15-20RM] Dumbbell bent over row [3 sets @ 15-20RM] Dumbbell curl [3 sets @ 15-20RM] Cable pushdown [3 sets @ 15-20RM] Leg curl [3 sets @ 15-20RM] Squat [3 sets @ 15-20RM] Crunch [3 sets @ 15-20RM] Calf raise [3 sets @ 15-20RM]
Tuesday	Rest	
Wednesday	Full Body	Dumbbell bench press [3 sets @ 15-20RM] Dumbbell military press [3 sets @ 15-20RM] Dumbbell bent over row [3 sets @ 15-20RM] Dumbbell curl [3 sets @ 15-20RM] Cable pushdown [3 sets @ 15-20RM] Leg curl [3 sets @ 15-20RM] Squat [3 sets @ 15-20RM] Crunch [3 sets @ 15-20RM] Calf raise [3 sets @ 15-20RM]
Thursday	Rest	
Friday	Full Body	Dumbbell bench press [3 sets @ 15-20RM] Dumbbell military press [3 sets @ 15-20RM] Dumbbell bent over row [3 sets @ 15-20RM] Dumbbell curl [3 sets @ 15-20RM] Cable pushdown [3 sets @ 15-20RM] Leg curl [3 sets @ 15-20RM] Squat [3 sets @ 15-20RM] Crunch [3 sets @ 15-20RM] Calf raise [3 sets @ 15-20RM]
Saturday	Rest	Aerobic Activity
Sunday	Rest	

Adaptation phase. Section 1. Week 3
Perceived effort level 8

DAY	MUSCLES	EXERCICES
Monday	Full Body	Dumbbell bench press [3 sets @ 15-20RM] Dumbbell military press [3 sets @ 15-20RM] Dumbbell bent over row [3 sets @ 15-20RM] Dumbbell curl [3 sets @ 15-20RM] Cable pushdown [3 sets @ 15-20RM] Leg curl [3 sets @ 15-20RM] Squat [3 sets @ 15-20RM] Crunch [3 sets @ 15-20RM] Calf raise [3 sets @ 15-20RM]
Tuesday	Rest	
Wednesday	Full Body	Dumbbell bench press [3 sets @ 15-20RM] Dumbbell military press [3 sets @ 15-20RM] Dumbbell bent over row [3 sets @ 15-20RM] Dumbbell curl [3 sets @ 15-20RM] Cable pushdown [3 sets @ 15-20RM] Leg curl [3 sets @ 15-20RM] Squat [3 sets @ 15-20RM] Crunch [3 sets @ 15-20RM] Calf raise [3 sets @ 15-20RM]
Thursday	Rest	
Friday	Full Body	Dumbbell bench press [3 sets @ 15-20RM] Dumbbell military press [3 sets @ 15-20RM] Dumbbell bent over row [3 sets @ 15-20RM] Dumbbell curl [3 sets @ 15-20RM] Cable pushdown [3 sets @ 15-20RM] Leg curl [3 sets @ 15-20RM] Squat [3 sets @ 15-20RM] Crunch [3 sets @ 15-20RM] Calf raise [3 sets @ 15-20RM]
Saturday	Rest	Aerobic Activity
Sunday	Rest	

=== **Woman and Fitness** ===

Adaptation phase. Section 1. Week 4
Perceived effort equal to 7

DAY	MUSCLES	EXERCICES
Monday	Full Body	Dumbbell bench press [3 sets @ 15-20RM] Dumbbell military press [3 sets @ 15-20RM] Dumbbell bent over row [3 sets @ 15-20RM] Dumbbell curl [3 sets @ 15-20RM] Cable pushdown [3 sets @ 15-20RM] Leg curl [3 sets @ 15-20RM] Squat [3 sets @ 15-20RM] Crunch [3 sets @ 15-20RM] Calf raise [3 sets @ 15-20RM]
Tuesday	Rest	
Wednesday	Full Body	Dumbbell bench press [3 sets @ 15-20RM] Dumbbell military press [3 sets @ 15-20RM] Dumbbell bent over row [3 sets @ 15-20RM] Dumbbell curl [3 sets @ 15-20RM] Cable pushdown [3 sets @ 15-20RM] Leg curl [3 sets @ 15-20RM] Squat [3 sets @ 15-20RM] Crunch [3 sets @ 15-20RM] Calf raise [3 sets @ 15-20RM]
Thursday	Rest	
Friday	Full Body	Dumbbell bench press [3 sets @ 15-20RM] Dumbbell military press [3 sets @ 15-20RM] Dumbbell bent over row [3 sets @ 15-20RM] Dumbbell curl [3 sets @ 15-20RM] Cable pushdown [3 sets @ 15-20RM] Leg curl [3 sets @ 15-20RM] Squat [3 sets @ 15-20RM] Crunch [3 sets @ 15-20RM] Calf raise [3 sets @ 15-20RM]
Saturday	Rest	Aerobic Activity
Sunday	Rest	

Adaptation phase. Section 2. Week 5

Perceived effort level 7, increase the weight after each set, the last until muscle failure

DAY	MUSCLES	EXERCICES
Monday	Full Body	Dumbbell bench press [3 sets @ 15-20RM] Dumbbell military press [3 sets @ 15-20RM] Low pulley row [3 sets @ 15-20RM] Dumbbell curl [3 sets @ 15-20RM] Cable pushdown [3 sets @ 15-20RM] Leg curl [3 sets @ 15-20RM] Leg extension [3 sets @ 15-20RM] Crunch [3 sets @ 15-20RM] Calf raise [3 sets @ 15-20RM]
Tuesday	Rest	
Wednesday	Full Body	Dumbbell bench press [3 sets @ 15-20RM] Dumbbell military press [3 sets @ 15-20RM] Low pulley row [3 sets @ 15-20RM] Dumbbell curl [3 sets @ 15-20RM] Cable pushdown [3 sets @ 15-20RM] Leg curl [3 sets @ 15-20RM] Leg extension [3 sets @ 15-20RM] Crunch [3 sets @ 15-20RM] Calf raise [3 sets @ 15-20RM]
Thursday	Rest	
Friday	Full Body	Dumbbell bench press [3 sets @ 15-20RM] Dumbbell military press [3 sets @ 15-20RM] Low pulley row [3 sets @ 15-20RM] Dumbbell curl [3 sets @ 15-20RM] Cable pushdown [3 sets @ 15-20RM] Leg curl [3 sets @ 15-20RM] Leg extension [3 sets @ 15-20RM] Crunch [3 sets @ 15-20RM] Calf raise [3 sets @ 15-20RM]
Saturday	Rest	Aerobic Activity
Sunday	Rest	

=== Woman and Fitness ===

Adaptation phase. Section 2. Week 6
Perceived effort level 7, increase the weight after each set, the last until muscle failure

DAY	MUSCLES	EXERCICES
Monday	Full Body	Dumbbell bench press [3 sets @ 10-12RM] Dumbbell military press [3 sets @ 10-12RM] Low pulley row [3 sets @ 10-12RM] Dumbbell curl [3 sets @ 10-12RM] Cable pushdown [3 sets @ 10-12RM] Leg curl [3 sets @ 10-12RM] Leg extension [3 sets @ 10-12RM] Crunch [3 sets @ 10-12RM] Calf raise [3 sets @ 10-12RM]
Tuesday	Rest	
Wednesday	Full Body	Dumbbell bench press [3 sets @ 10-12RM] Dumbbell military press [3 sets @ 10-12RM] Low pulley row [3 sets @ 10-12RM] Dumbbell curl [3 sets @ 10-12RM] Cable pushdown [3 sets @ 10-12RM] Leg curl [3 sets @ 10-12RM] Leg extension [3 sets @ 10-12RM] Crunch [3 sets @ 10-12RM] Calf raise [3 sets @ 10-12RM]
Thursday	Rest	
Friday	Full Body	Dumbbell bench press [3 sets @ 10-12RM] Dumbbell military press [3 sets @ 10-12RM] Low pulley row [3 sets @ 10-12RM] Dumbbell curl [3 sets @ 10-12RM] Cable pushdown [3 sets @ 10-12RM] Leg curl [3 sets @ 10-12RM] Leg extension [3 sets @ 10-12RM] Crunch [3 sets @ 10-12RM] Calf raise [3 sets @ 10-12RM]
Saturday	Rest	Aerobic Activity
Sunday	Rest	

Adaptation phase. Section 2. Week 7
Perceived effort level 7, increase the weight after each set, the last until muscle failure

DAY	MUSCLES	EXERCICES
Monday	Full Body	Dumbbell bench press [3 sets @ 8-10RM] Dumbbell military press [3 sets @ 8-10RM] Low pulley row [3 sets @ 8-10RM] Dumbbell curl [3 sets @ 8-10RM] Cable pushdown [3 sets @ 8-10RM] Leg curl [3 sets @ 8-10RM] Leg extension [3 sets @ 8-10RM] Crunch [3 sets @ 8-10RM] Calf raise [3 sets @ 8-10RM]
Tuesday	Rest	
Wednesday	Full Body	Dumbbell bench press [3 sets @ 8-10RM] Dumbbell military press [3 sets @ 8-10RM] Low pulley row [3 sets @ 8-10RM] Dumbbell curl [3 sets @ 8-10RM] Cable pushdown [3 sets @ 8-10RM] Leg curl [3 sets @ 8-10RM] Leg extension [3 sets @ 8-10RM] Crunch [3 sets @ 8-10RM] Calf raise [3 sets @ 8-10RM]
Thursday	Rest	
Friday	Full Body	Dumbbell bench press [3 sets @ 8-10RM] Dumbbell military press [3 sets @ 8-10RM] Low pulley row [3 sets @ 8-10RM] Dumbbell curl [3 sets @ 8-10RM] Cable pushdown [3 sets @ 8-10RM] Leg curl [3 sets @ 8-10RM] Leg extension [3 sets @ 8-10RM] Crunch [3 sets @ 8-10RM] Calf raise [3 sets @ 8-10RM]
Saturday	Rest	Aerobic Activity
Sunday	Rest	

=== Woman and Fitness ===

Adaptation phase. Section 2. Week 8
Perceived effort level 7, increase the weight after each set, the last until muscle failure

DAY	MUSCLES	EXERCICES
Monday	Full Body	Dumbbell bench press [3 sets @ 15-20RM] Dumbbell military press [3 sets @ 15-20RM] Low pulley row [3 sets @ 15-20RM] Dumbbell curl [3 sets @ 15-20RM] Cable pushdown [3 sets @ 15-20RM] Leg curl [3 sets @ 15-20RM] Leg extension [3 sets @ 15-20RM] Crunch [3 sets @ 15-20RM] Calf raise [3 sets @ 15-20RM]
Tuesday	Rest	
Wednesday	Full Body	Dumbbell bench press [3 sets @ 15-20RM] Dumbbell military press [3 sets @ 15-20RM] Low pulley row [3 sets @ 15-20RM] Dumbbell curl [3 sets @ 15-20RM] Cable pushdown [3 sets @ 15-20RM] Leg curl [3 sets @ 15-20RM] Leg extension [3 sets @ 15-20RM] Crunch [3 sets @ 15-20RM] Calf raise [3 sets @ 15-20RM]
Thursday	Rest	
Friday	Full Body	Dumbbell bench press [3 sets @ 15-20RM] Dumbbell military press [3 sets @ 15-20RM] Low pulley row [3 sets @ 15-20RM] Dumbbell curl [3 sets @ 15-20RM] Cable pushdown [3 sets @ 15-20RM] Leg curl [3 sets @ 15-20RM] Leg extension [3 sets @ 15-20RM] Crunch [3 sets @ 15-20RM] Calf raise [3 sets @ 15-20RM]
Saturday	Rest	Aerobic Activity
Sunday	Rest	

Strength phase (8 weeks)

This phase is divided into two mesocycles of four weeks each, in which you train with high loads and with low repetitions, the rests between one series and the next are about 2-3 minutes.
In the first mesocycle, you train three days a week in full-body, in the second at least four but with split routines.

=== Woman and Fitness ===

Strength phase. Section 1. Week 1
Perceived effort level 8, increase the weight after each set, the last until muscle failure

DAY	MUSCLES	EXERCICES
Monday	Full Body	Bench press [3 sets @ 5-6 RM] Military press [3 sets @ 5-6 RM] Low pulley row [3 sets @ 5-6 RM] Dumbbell curl [3 sets @ 5-6 RM] Cable pushdown [3 sets @ 5-6 RM] Leg curl [3 sets @ 5-6 RM] Squat [3 sets @ 5-6 RM] Crunch [3 sets @ 15-20RM]
Tuesday	Rest	
Wednesday	Full Body	Bench press [3 sets @ 5-6 RM] Military press [3 sets @ 5-6 RM] Low pulley row [3 sets @ 5-6 RM] Dumbbell curl [3 sets @ 5-6 RM] Cable pushdown [3 sets @ 5-6 RM] Leg curl [3 sets @ 5-6 RM] Squat [3 sets @ 5-6 RM] Crunch [3 sets @ 15-20RM]
Thursday	Rest	
Friday	Full Body	Bench press [3 sets @ 5-6 RM] Military press [3 sets @ 5-6 RM] Low pulley row [3 sets @ 5-6 RM] Dumbbell curl [3 sets @ 5-6 RM] Cable pushdown [3 sets @ 5-6 RM] Leg curl [3 sets @ 5-6 RM] Squat [3 sets @ 5-6 RM] Crunch [3 sets @ 15-20RM]
Saturday	Rest	Aerobic Activity
Sunday	Rest	

Strength phase. Section 1. Week 2
Perceived effort level 8, increase the weight after each set, the last until muscle failure

DAY	MUSCLES	EXERCICES
Monday	Full Body	Bench press [3 sets @ 3-5 RM] Military press [3 sets @ 3-5 RM] Low pulley row [3 sets @ 3-5 RM] Dumbbell curl [3 sets @ 3-5 RM] Cable pushdown [3 sets @ 3-5 RM] Leg curl [3 sets @ 3-5 RM] Squat [3 sets @ 3-5 RM] Crunch [3 sets @ 15-20RM]
Tuesday	Rest	
Wednesday	Full Body	Bench press [3 sets @ 3-5 RM] Military press [3 sets @ 3-5 RM] Low pulley row [3 sets @ 3-5 RM] Dumbbell curl [3 sets @ 3-5 RM] Cable pushdown [3 sets @ 3-5 RM] Leg curl [3 sets @ 3-5 RM] Squat [3 sets @ 3-5 RM] Crunch [3 sets @ 15-20RM]
Thursday	Rest	
Friday	Full Body	Bench press [3 sets @ 3-5 RM] Military press [3 sets @ 3-5 RM] Low pulley row [3 sets @ 3-5 RM] Dumbbell curl [3 sets @ 3-5 RM] Cable pushdown [3 sets @ 3-5 RM] Leg curl [3 sets @ 3-5 RM] Squat [3 sets @ 3-5 RM] Crunch [3 sets @ 15-20RM]
Saturday	Rest	Aerobic Activity
Sunday	Rest	

=== **Woman and Fitness** ===

Strength phase. Section 1. Week 3

Perceived effort level 8, increase the weight after each set, the last until muscle failure

DAY	MUSCLES	EXERCICES
Monday	Full Body	Bench press [3 sets @ 1-3 RM] Military press [3 sets @ 1-3 RM] Low pulley row [3 sets @ 1-3 RM] Dumbbell curl [3 sets @ 1-3 RM] Cable pushdown [3 sets @ 1-3 RM] Leg curl [3 sets @ 1-3 RM] Squat [3 sets @ 1-3 RM] Crunch [3 sets @ 15-20RM]
Tuesday	Rest	
Wednesday	Full Body	Bench press [3 sets @ 1-3 RM] Military press [3 sets @ 1-3 RM] Low pulley row [3 sets @ 1-3 RM] Dumbbell curl [3 sets @ 1-3 RM] Cable pushdown [3 sets @ 1-3 RM] Leg curl [3 sets @ 1-3 RM] Squat [3 sets @ 1-3 RM] Crunch [3 sets @ 15-20RM]
Thursday	Rest	
Friday	Full Body	Bench press [3 sets @ 1-3 RM] Military press [3 sets @ 1-3 RM] Low pulley row [3 sets @ 1-3 RM] Dumbbell curl [3 sets @ 1-3 RM] Cable pushdown [3 sets @ 1-3 RM] Leg curl [3 sets @ 1-3 RM] Squat [3 sets @ 1-3 RM] Crunch [3 sets @ 15-20RM]
Saturday	Rest	Aerobic Activity
Sunday	Rest	

[215]

Strength phase. Section 1. Week 4

Perceived effort level 7, increase the weight after each set, the last until muscle failure

DAY	MUSCLES	EXERCICES
Monday	Full Body	Bench press [3 sets @ 10-12 RM] Military press [3 sets @ 10-12 RM] Low pulley row [3 sets @ 10-12 RM] Dumbbell curl [3 sets @ 10-12 RM] Cable pushdown [3 sets @ 10-12 RM] Leg curl [3 sets @ 10-12 RM] Squat [3 sets @ 10-12 RM] Crunch [3 sets @ 15-20RM]
Tuesday	Rest	
Wednesday	Full Body	Bench press [3 sets @ 10-12 RM] Military press [3 sets @ 10-12 RM] Low pulley row [3 sets @ 10-12 RM] Dumbbell curl [3 sets @ 10-12 RM] Cable pushdown [3 sets @ 10-12 RM] Leg curl [3 sets @ 10-12 RM] Squat [3 sets @ 10-12 RM] Crunch [3 sets @ 15-20RM]
Thursday	Rest	
Friday	Full Body	Bench press [3 sets @ 10-12 RM] Military press [3 sets @ 10-12 RM] Low pulley row [3 sets @ 10-12 RM] Dumbbell curl [3 sets @ 10-12 RM] Cable pushdown [3 sets @ 10-12 RM] Leg curl [3 sets @ 10-12 RM] Squat [3 sets @ 10-12 RM] Crunch [3 sets @ 15-20RM]
Saturday	Rest	Aerobic Activity
Sunday	Rest	

=== Woman and Fitness ===

Strength phase. Section 2. Week 5
Perceived effort level 7, increase the weight after each set, the last until muscle failure

DAY	MUSCLES	EXERCICES
Monday	Upper Body	Bench press [3 sets @ 6-8 RM] Military press [3 sets @ 6-8 RM] Dumbbell flyes [3 sets @ 6-8 RM] Lat machine [3 sets @ 6-8 RM] Dumbbell curl [3 sets @ 6-8 RM] Cable pushdown [3 sets @ 6-8 RM]
Tuesday	Lower Body	Leg curl [3 sets @ 6-8 RM] Squat [3 sets @ 6-8 RM] Calf raise [3 sets @ 6-8 RM] Crunch [3 sets @ 15-20RM]
Wednesday	Rest	
Thursday	Upper Body	Bench press [3 sets @ 6-8 RM] Military press [3 sets @ 6-8 RM] Lateral raises [3 sets @ 6-8 RM] Lat machine [3 sets @ 6-8 RM] Dumbbell curl [3 sets @ 6-8 RM] Cable pushdown [3 sets @ 6-8 RM]
Friday	Lower Body	Leg curl [3 sets @ 6-8 RM] Squat [3 sets @ 6-8 RM] Calf raise [3 sets @ 6-8 RM] Crunch [3 sets @ 15-20RM]
Saturday	Rest	Aerobic Activity
Sunday	Rest	

Strength phase. Section 2. Week 6
Perceived effort level 8 increase the weight after each set, the last until muscle failure

DAY	MUSCLES	EXERCICES
Monday	Upper Body	Bench press [3 sets @ 3-5 RM] Military press [3 sets @ 3-5 RM] Dumbbell flyes [3 sets @ 3-5 RM] Lat machine [3 sets @ 3-5 RM] Dumbbell curl [3 sets @ 3-5 RM] Cable pushdown [3 sets @ 3-5 RM]
Tuesday	Lower Body	Leg curl [3 sets @ 3-5 RM] Squat [3 sets @ 3-5 RM] Calf raise [3 sets @ 3-5 RM] Crunch [3 sets @ 15-20RM]
Wednesday	Rest	
Thursday	Upper Body	Bench press [3 sets @ 3-5 RM] Military press [3 sets @ 3-5 RM] Lateral raises [3 serie @3-5 RM] Lat machine [3 sets @ 3-5 RM] Dumbbell curl [3 sets @ 3-5 RM] Cable pushdown [3 sets @ 3-5 RM]
Friday	Lower Body	Leg curl [3 sets @ 3-5 RM] Squat [3 sets @ 3-5 RM] Calf raise [3 sets @ 3-5 RM] Crunch [3 sets @ 15-20RM]
Saturday	Rest	Aerobic Activity
Sunday	Rest	

=== Woman and Fitness ===

Strength phase. Section 2. Week 7
Perceived effort level 9, increase the weight after each set, the last until muscle failure

DAY	MUSCLES	EXERCICES
Monday	Upper Body	Bench press [3 sets @ 2-3 RM] Military press [3 sets @ 2-3 RM] Dumbbell flyes [3 sets @ 2-3 RM] Lat machine [3 sets @ 2-3 RM] Dumbbell curl [3 sets @ 2-3 RM] Cable pushdown [3 sets @ 2-3 RM]
Tuesday	Lower Body	Leg curl [3 sets @ 2-3 RM] Squat [3 sets @ 2-3 RM] Calf raise [3 sets @ 2-3 RM] Crunch [3 sets @ 15-20RM]
Wednesday	Rest	
Thursday	Upper Body	Bench press [3 sets @ 2-3 RM] Military press [3 sets @ 2-3 RM] Lateral raises [3 serie @2-3 RM] Lat machine [3 sets @ 2-3 RM] Dumbbell curl [3 sets @ 2-3 RM] Cable pushdown [3 sets @ 2-3 RM]
Friday	Lower Body	Leg curl [3 sets @ 2-3 RM] Squat [3 sets @ 2-3 RM] Calf raise [3 sets @ 2-3 RM] Crunch [3 sets @ 15-20RM]
Saturday	Rest	Aerobic Activity
Sunday	Rest	

Strength phase. Section 2. Week 8

Perceived effort level 7, increase the weight after each set, the last until muscle failure

DAY	MUSCLES	EXERCICES
Monday	Upper Body	Bench press [3 sets @ 10-12 RM] Military press [3 sets @ 10-12 RM] Dumbbell flyes [3 sets @ 10-12RM] Lat machine [3 sets @ 10-12 RM] Dumbbell curl [3 sets @ 10-12 RM] Cable pushdown [3 sets @ 10-12 RM]
Tuesday	Lower Body	Leg curl [3 sets @ 10-12 RM] Squat [3 sets @ 10-12 RM] Calf raise [3 sets @ 10-12 RM] Crunch [3 sets @ 15-20RM]
Wednesday	Rest	
Thursday	Upper Body	Bench press [3 sets @ 10-12 RM] Military press [3 sets @ 10-12 RM] Dumbbell flyes [3 sets @ 10-12 RM] Lat machine [3 sets @ 10-12 RM] Dumbbell curl [3 sets @ 10-12 RM] Cable pushdown [3 sets @ 10-12 RM]
Friday	Lower Body	Leg curl [3 sets @ 10-12 RM] Squat [3 sets @ 10-12 RM] Calf raise [3 sets @ 10-12 RM] Crunch [3 sets @ 15-20RM]
Saturday	Rest	Aerobic Activity
Sunday	Rest	

Recovery phase (4 weeks)

In this mesocycle we increase the repetitions by decreasing the maximum weight used, this gives the body the time it needs to recover after the strength phase, which was a period of intense work. At the same time, we reduce the recovery time between one set and the next to increase metabolic work. This procedure can also be used in protocols for body definition or slimming in combination with a low-calorie diet.

Recovery phase. Week 1
Perceived effort equal to 7, rest 30-45 sec. between sets

DAY	MUSCLES	EXERCICES
Monday	Full Body	Dumbbell bench press [3 sets @ 15-20RM] Dumbbell military press [3 sets @ 15-20RM] Low pulley row [3 sets @ 15-20RM] Dumbbell curl [3 sets @ 15-20RM] Cable pushdown [3 sets @ 15-20RM] Leg curl [3 sets @ 15-20RM] Leg extension [3 sets @ 15-20RM] Crunch [3 sets @ 15-20RM] Calf raise [3 sets @ 15-20RM]
Tuesday	Rest	
Wednesday	Full Body	Dumbbell flyes [3 sets @ 10-12RM] Lateral raises[3 sets @ 110-12RM] Low pulley row [3 sets @ 10-12RM] Dumbbell curl [3 sets @ 10-12RM] Cable pushdown [3 sets @ 10-12RM] Leg curl [3 sets @ 10-12RM] Leg extension [3 sets @ 10-12RM] Crunch [3 sets @ 10-12RM] Calf raise [3 sets @ 10-12RM]
Thursday	Rest	
Friday	Full Body	Dumbbell bench press [3 sets @ 15-20RM] Dumbbell military press [3 sets @ 15-20RM] Low pulley row [3 sets @ 15-20RM] Dumbbell curl [3 sets @ 15-20RM] Cable pushdown [3 sets @ 15-20RM] Leg curl [3 sets @ 15-20RM] Leg extension [3 sets @ 15-20RM] Crunch [3 sets @ 15-20RM] Calf raise [3 sets @ 15-20RM]
Saturday	Rest	
Sunday	Rest	

=== **Woman and Fitness** ===

Recovery phase. Week 2
Perceived effort equal to-7, rest 30-45 sec. between sets

DAY	MUSCLES	EXERCICES
Monday	Full Body	Dumbbell bench press [3 sets @ 15-20RM] Dumbbell military press [3 sets @ 15-20RM] Lat Machine [3 sets @ 15-20RM] Dumbbell curl [3 sets @ 15-20RM] Cable pushdown [3 sets @ 15-20RM] Leg curl [3 sets @ 15-20RM] Leg press [3 sets @ 15-20RM] Crunch [3 sets @ 15-20RM] Calf raise [3 sets @ 15-20RM]
Tuesday	Rest	
Wednesday	Full Body	Dumbbell flyes [3 sets @ 10-12RM] Lateral raises[3 sets @ 110-12RM] Low pulley row [3 sets @ 10-12RM] Dumbbell curl [3 sets @ 10-12RM] Cable pushdown [3 sets @ 10-12RM] Leg curl [3 sets @ 10-12RM] Leg extension [3 sets @ 10-12RM] Crunch [3 sets @ 10-12RM] Calf raise [3 sets @ 10-12RM]
Thursday	Rest	
Friday	Full Body	Dumbbell bench press [3 sets @ 15-20RM] Dumbbell military press [3 sets @ 15-20RM] Lat Machine [3 sets @ 15-20RM] Dumbbell curl [3 sets @ 15-20RM] Cable pushdown [3 sets @ 15-20RM] Leg curl [3 sets @ 15-20RM] Leg press [3 sets @ 15-20RM] Crunch [3 sets @ 15-20RM] Calf raise [3 sets @ 15-20RM]
Saturday	Rest	
Sunday	Rest	

Recovery phase. Week 3
Perceived effort equal to-7, rest 30-45 sec. between sets

DAY	MUSCLES	EXERCICES
Monday	Full Body	Dumbbell bench press [3 sets @ 15-20RM] Dumbbell military press [3 sets @ 15-20RM] Low pulley row [3 sets @ 15-20RM] Dumbbell curl [3 sets @ 15-20RM] Cable pushdown [3 sets @ 15-20RM] Leg curl [3 sets @ 15-20RM] Leg extension [3 sets @ 15-20RM] Crunch [3 sets @ 15-20RM] Calf raise [3 sets @ 15-20RM]
Tuesday	Rest	
Wednesday	Full Body	Dumbbell flyes [3 sets @ 10-12RM] Lateral raises[3 sets @ 110-12RM] Low pulley row [3 sets @ 10-12RM] Dumbbell curl [3 sets @ 10-12RM] Cable pushdown [3 sets @ 10-12RM] Leg curl [3 sets @ 10-12RM] Leg extension [3 sets @ 10-12RM] Crunch [3 sets @ 10-12RM] Calf raise [3 sets @ 10-12RM]
Thursday	Rest	
Friday	Full Body	Dumbbell bench press [3 sets @ 15-20RM] Dumbbell military press [3 sets @ 15-20RM] Low pulley row [3 sets @ 15-20RM] Dumbbell curl [3 sets @ 15-20RM] Cable pushdown [3 sets @ 15-20RM] Leg curl [3 sets @ 15-20RM] Leg extension [3 sets @ 15-20RM] Crunch [3 sets @ 15-20RM] Calf raise [3 sets @ 15-20RM]
Saturday	Rest	
Sunday	Rest	

=== Woman and Fitness ===

Recovery phase. Week 4.
Perceived effort equal to-7, rest 30-45 sec. between sets

DAY	MUSCLES	EXERCICES
Monday	Full Body	Dumbbell bench press [3 sets @ 15-20RM] Dumbbell military press [3 sets @ 15-20RM] Lat Machine [3 sets @ 15-20RM] Dumbbell curl [3 sets @ 15-20RM] Cable pushdown [3 sets @ 15-20RM] Leg curl [3 sets @ 15-20RM] Leg press [3 sets @ 15-20RM] Crunch [3 sets @ 15-20RM] Calf raise [3 sets @ 15-20RM]
Tuesday	Rest	
Wednesday	Full Body	Dumbbell flyes [3 sets @ 15-20RM] Lateral raises[3 sets @ 15-20RM] Low pulley row [3 sets @ 15-20RM] Dumbbell curl [3 sets @ 15-20RM] Cable pushdown [3 sets @ 15-20RM] Leg curl [3 sets @ 15-20RM] Leg extension [3 sets @ 15-20RM] Crunch [3 sets @ 15-20RM] Calf raise [3 sets @ 15-20RM]
Thursday	Rest	
Friday	Full Body	Dumbbell bench press [3 sets @ 15-20RM] Dumbbell military press [3 sets @ 15-20RM] Lat Machine [3 sets @ 15-20RM] Dumbbell curl [3 sets @ 15-20RM] Cable pushdown [3 sets @ 15-20RM] Leg curl [3 sets @ 15-20RM] Leg press [3 sets @ 15-20RM] Crunch [3 sets @ 15-20RM] Calf raise [3 sets @ 15-20RM]
Saturday	Rest	
Sunday	Rest	

Hypertrophy phase (12 weeks)

In this phase, we will seek maximum muscle development. It is divided into three mesocycles of four weeks.

Medium to high loads will be used to allow 6 to 12 repetitions; the rest between sets will be 60-90 seconds.

The repetitions must always be performed in full control of the movement.

The first mesocycle is in full-body over three days. The second and third mesocycles are based on a 5-day split routine.

The weight will be increased after each week excluding the last week of each mesocycle to allow adequate recovery without losing muscle tone.

=== The Shape Of Body To Come ===

Hypertrophy phase. Mesocycle 1. Week 1

DAY	MUSCLES	EXERCICES
Monday	Full Body	Dumbbell bench press [3 sets @ 10-12RM] Dumbbell military press [3 sets @ 10-12RM] Low pulley row [3 sets @ 10-12RM] Dumbbell curl [3 sets @ 10-12RM] Cable pushdown [3 sets @ 10-12RM] Leg curl [3 sets @ 10-12RM] Leg extension [3 sets @ 10-12RM] Crunch [3 sets @ 10-12RM] Calf raise [3 sets @ 10-12RM]
Tuesday	Rest	
Wednesday	Full Body	Dumbbell flyes [3 sets @ 10-12RM] Lateral raises [3 sets @ 10-12RM] Lat Machine [3 sets @ 10-12RM] Dumbbell curl [3 sets @ 10-12RM] Cable pushdown [3 sets @ 10-12RM] Leg curl [3 sets @ 10-12RM] Leg extension [3 sets @ 10-12RM] Crunch [3 sets @ 10-12RM] Calf raise [3 sets @ 10-12RM]
Thursday	Rest	
Friday	Full Body	Dumbbell bench press [3 sets @ 10-12RM] Dumbbell military press [3 sets @ 10-12RM] Low pulley row [3 sets @ 10-12RM] Dumbbell curl [3 sets @ 10-12RM] Cable pushdown [3 sets @ 10-12RM] Leg curl [3 sets @ 10-12RM] Leg extension [3 sets @ 10-12RM] Crunch [3 sets @ 10-12RM] Calf raise [3 sets @ 10-12RM]
Saturday	Rest	Aerobic Activity
Sunday	Rest	

Hypertrophy phase. Mesocycle 1. Week 2

DAY	MUSCLES	EXERCICES
Monday	Full Body	Dumbbell bench press [3 sets @ 8-10RM] Dumbbell military press [3 sets @ 1 8-10RM] Low pulley row [3 sets @ 8-10RM] Dumbbell curl [3 sets @ 8-10RM] Cable pushdown [3 sets @ 8-10RM] Leg curl [3 sets @ 8-10RM] Leg extension [3 sets @ 8-10RM] Crunch [3 sets @ 8-10RM] Calf raise [3 sets @ 8-10RM]
Tuesday	Rest	
Wednesday	Full Body	Dumbbell flyes [3 sets @ 8-10RM] Lateral raises [3 sets @ 8-10RM] Lat Machine [3 sets @ 8-10RM] Dumbbell curl [3 sets @ 8-10RM] Cable pushdown [3 sets @ 8-10RM] Leg curl [3 sets @ 8-10RM] Leg extension [3 sets @ 8-10RM] Crunch [3 sets @ 8-10RM] Calf raise [3 sets @ 8-10RM]
Thursday	Rest	
Friday	Full Body	Dumbbell bench press [3 sets @ 8-10RM] Dumbbell military press [3 sets @ 1 8-10RM] Low pulley row [3 sets @ 8-10RM] Dumbbell curl [3 sets @ 8-10RM] Cable pushdown [3 sets @ 8-10RM] Leg curl [3 sets @ 8-10RM] Leg extension [3 sets @ 8-10RM] Crunch [3 sets @ 8-10RM] Calf raise [3 sets @ 8-10RM]
Saturday	Rest	Aerobic Activity
Sunday	Rest	

=== Woman and Fitness ===

Hypertrophy phase. Mesocycle 1. Week 3

Loads are increased and repetitions reduced, always with maximum control of movement. Recovery between one set and another of 60 secs..

DAY	MUSCLES	EXERCICES
Monday	Full Body	Dumbbell bench press [3 sets @ 6-8RM] Dumbbell military press [3 sets @ 6-8RM] Low pulley row [3 sets @ 6-8RM] Dumbbell curl [3 sets @ 6-8 RM] Cable pushdown [3 sets @ 6-8RM] Leg curl [3 sets @ 6-8RM] Leg extension [3 sets @ 6-8RM] Crunch [3 sets @ 6-8RM] Calf raise [3 sets @ 6-8RM]
Tuesday	Rest	
Wednesday	Full Body	Dumbbell flyes [3 sets @ 6-8RM] Lateral raises [3 sets @ 6-8RM] Lat Machine [3 sets @ 6-8RM] Dumbbell curl [3 sets @ 6-8RM] Cable pushdown [3 sets @ 6-8RM] Leg curl [3 sets @ 6-8RM] Leg extension [3 sets @ 6-8RM] Crunch [3 sets @ 6-8RM] Calf raise [3 sets @ 6-8RM]
Thursday	Rest	
Friday	Full Body	Dumbbell bench press [3 sets @ 6-8RM] Dumbbell military press [3 sets @ 6-8RM] Low pulley row [3 sets @ 6-8RM] Dumbbell curl [3 sets @ 6-8 RM] Cable pushdown [3 sets @ 6-8RM] Leg curl [3 sets @ 6-8RM] Leg extension [3 sets @ 6-8RM] Crunch [3 sets @ 6-8RM] Calf raise [3 sets @ 6-8RM]
Saturday	Rest	Aerobic Activity
Sunday	Rest	

[229]

=== **Andrea Raimondi** ===

Hypertrophy phase. Mesocycle 1. Week 4
Week unloading before the new Mesocycle, decrease loads and increase repetitions, rest 45-60 "

DAY	MUSCLES	EXERCICES
Monday	Full Body	Dumbbell bench press [3 sets @ 10-12RM] Dumbbell military press [3 sets @ 10-12RM] Low pulley row [3 sets @ 10-12RM] Dumbbell curl [3 sets @ 10-12RM] Cable pushdown [3 sets @ 10-12RM] Leg curl [3 sets @ 10-12RM] Leg extension [3 sets @ 10-12RM] Crunch [3 sets @ 10-12RM] Calf raise [3 sets @ 10-12RM]
Tuesday	Rest	
Wednesday	Full Body	Dumbbell flyes [3 sets @ 10-12RM] Lateral raises [3 sets @ 10-12RM] Lat Machine [3 sets @ 10-12RM] Dumbbell curl [3 sets @ 10-12RM] Cable pushdown [3 sets @ 10-12RM] Leg curl [3 sets @ 10-12RM] Leg extension [3 sets @ 10-12RM] Crunch [3 sets @ 10-12RM] Calf raise [3 sets @ 10-12RM]
Thursday	Rest	
Friday	Full Body	Dumbbell bench press [3 sets @ 10-12RM] Dumbbell military press [3 sets @ 10-12RM] Low pulley row [3 sets @ 10-12RM] Dumbbell curl [3 sets @ 10-12RM] Cable pushdown [3 sets @ 10-12RM] Leg curl [3 sets @ 10-12RM] Leg extension [3 sets @ 10-12RM] Crunch [3 sets @ 10-12RM] Calf raise [3 sets @ 10-12RM]
Saturday	Rest	Aerobic Activity
Sunday	Rest	

=== **Woman and Fitness** ===

Hypertrophy phase. Mesocycle 2. Week 5.

DAY	MUSCLES	EXERCICES
Monday	Chest, Back, Legs, Abdominals	Dumbbell bench press [4 sets @ 10-12RM] Dumbbell flyes [4 sets @ 10-12RM] Low pulley row [4 sets @ 10-12RM] Leg curl [4 sets @ 10-12RM] Crunch [4 sets @ 10-12RM]
Tuesday	Shoulders, Legs, Abdominals	Military press [4 sets @ 10-12RM] Lateral raises [4 sets @ 10-12RM] Rear lateral raises [4 sets @ 10-12RM] Leg extension [4 sets @ 10-12RM] Leg Press [4 sets @ 10-12RM] Calf raise [4 sets @ 10-12RM] Crunch [4 sets @ 10-12RM]
Wednesday	Arms, Abdominals	Dumbbell curl [3 sets @ 10-12RM] Cable pushdown [3 sets @ 10-12RM] Crunch [4 sets @ 10-12RM]
Thursday	Chest, Back, Legs, Abdominals	Dumbbell bench press [4 sets @ 10-12RM] Dumbbell flyes [4 sets @ 10-12RM] Lat Machine [4 sets @ 10-12RM] Leg curl [4 sets @ 10-12RM] Crunch [4 sets @ 10-12RM]
Friday	Shoulders, Legs, Abdominals	Military press [4 sets @ 10-12RM] Lateral raises [4 sets @ 10-12RM] Rear lateral raises [4 sets @ 10-12RM] Leg extension [4 sets @ 10-12RM] Leg Press [4 sets @ 10-12RM] Calf raise [4 sets @ 10-12RM] Crunch [4 sets @ 10-12RM]
Saturday	Rest	Aerobic Activity
Sunday	Rest	

[231]

Hypertrophy phase. Mesocycle 2. Week 6.
Loads increase, rest 60-90 secs.

DAY	MUSCLES	EXERCICES
Monday	Chest, Back, Legs, Abdominals	Dumbbell bench press [4 sets @ 8-10RM] Dumbbell flyes [4 sets @ 8-10RM] Low pulley row [4 sets @ 8-10RM] Leg curl [4 sets @ 8-10RM] Crunch [4 sets @ 15-20RM]
Tuesday	Shoulders, Legs, Abdominals	Military press [4 sets @ 8-10RM] Lateral raises [4 sets @ 8-10RM] Rear lateral raises [4 sets @ 8-10RM] Leg extension [4 sets @ 8-10RM] Leg Press [4 sets @ 8-10RM] Calf raise [4 sets @ 8-10RM] Crunch [4 sets @ 15-20RM]
Wednesday	Arms, Abdominals	Dumbbell curl [4 sets @ 8-10RM] Cable pushdown [4 sets @ 8-10RM] Crunch [4 sets @ 8-10RM]
Thursday	Chest, Back, Legs, Abdominals	Dumbbell bench press [4 sets @ 8-10RM] Dumbbell flyes [4 sets @ 8-10RM] Lat Machine [4 sets @ 8-10RM] Leg curl [4 sets @ 8-10RM] Crunch [4 sets @ 15-20RM]
Friday	Shoulders, Legs, Abdominals	Military press [4 sets @ 8-10RM] Lateral raises [4 sets @ 8-10RM] Rear lateral raises [4 sets @ 8-10RM] Leg extension [4 sets @ 8-10RM] Leg Press [4 sets @ 8-10RM] Calf raise [4 sets @ 8-10RM] Crunch [4 sets @ 15-20RM]
Saturday	Rest	Aerobic Activity
Sunday	Rest	

=== Woman and Fitness ===

Hypertrophy phase. Mesocycle 2. Week 7.
The number of series is increased with a medium-high load, rest of 60-90 " between the sets

DAY	MUSCLES	EXERCICES
Monday	Chest, Back, Legs, Abdominals	Dumbbell bench press [5 sets @ 8-10 RM] Dumbbell flyes [5 sets @ 8-10 RM] Low pulley row [5 sets @ 8-10 RM] Leg curl [5 sets @ 8-10 RM] Crunch [4 sets @ 15-20 RM]
Tuesday	Shoulders, Legs, Abdominals	Military press [5 sets @ 8-10 RM] Lateral raises [5 sets @ 8-10 RM] Rear lateral raises [5 sets @ 8-10 RM] Leg extension [5 sets @ 8-10 RM] Leg Press [4 sets @ 8-10RM] Calf raise [5 sets @ 8-10 RM] Crunch [4 sets @ 15-20RM]
Wednesday	Arms, Abdominals	Dumbbell curl [5 sets @ 8-10RM] Cable pushdown [5 sets @ 8-10RM] Crunch [4 sets @ 15-20RM]
Thursday	Chest, Back, Legs, Abdominals	Dumbbell bench press [5 sets @ 8-10 RM] Dumbbell flyes [5 sets @ 8-10 RM] Lat Machine [5 sets @ 8-10 RM] Leg curl [5 sets @ 8-10 RM] Crunch [4 sets @ 15-20 RM]
Friday	Shoulders, Legs, Abdominals	Military press [5 sets @ 8-10 RM] Lateral raises [5 sets @ 8-10 RM] Rear lateral raises [5 sets @ 8-10 RM] Leg extension [5 sets @ 8-10 RM] Leg Press [4 sets @ 8-10RM] Calf raise [5 sets @ 8-10 RM] Crunch [4 sets @ 15-20RM]
Saturday	Rest	Aerobic Activity
Sunday	Rest	

Hypertrophy phase. Mesocycle 2. Week 8.
Unloading week, lower the loads, raise the repetitions, bring the recovery between one set and another to 45-60 secs

DAY	MUSCLES	EXERCICES
Monday	Chest, Back, Legs, Abdominals	Dumbbell bench press [4 sets @ 15-20RM] Dumbbell flyes [4 sets @ 15-20RM] Low pulley row [4 sets @ 15-20RM] Leg curl [4 sets @ 15-20RM] Crunch [4 sets @ 15-20RM]
Tuesday	Shoulders, Legs, Abdominals	Military press [4 sets @ 15-20RM] Lateral raises [4 sets @ 15-20RM] Rear lateral raises [4 sets @ 15-20RM] Leg extension [4 sets @ 15-20RM] Leg Press [4 sets @ 15-20RM] Calf raise [4 sets @ 15-20RM] Crunch [4 sets @ 15-20RM]
Wednesday	Arms, Abdominals	Dumbbell curl [3 sets @ 15-20RM] Cable pushdown [3 sets @ 15-20RM] Crunch [4 sets @ 15-20RM]
Thursday	Chest, Back, Legs, Abdominals	Dumbbell bench press [4 sets @ 15-20RM] Dumbbell flyes [4 sets @ 15-20RM] Lat Machine [4 sets @ 15-20RM] Leg curl [4 sets @ 15-20RM] Crunch [4 sets @ 15-20RM]
Friday	Shoulders, Legs, Abdominals	Military press [4 sets @ 15-20RM] Lateral raises [4 sets @ 15-20RM] Rear lateral raises [4 sets @ 15-20RM] Leg extension [4 sets @ 15-20RM] Leg Press [4 sets @ 15-20RM] Calf raise [4 sets @ 15-20RM] Crunch [4 sets @ 15-20RM]
Saturday	Rest	Aerobic Activity
Sunday	Rest	

=== **Woman and Fitness** ===

Hypertrophy phase. Mesocycle 3. Week 9.
The superset and triset techniques are used to hit the same muscle district with medium-high load. Superset and triset techniques are introduced. Rest of 60-90 secs between the sets

DAY	MUSCLES	EXERCICES
Monday	Chest, Back, Legs, Abdominals	Dumbbell bench press [4 sets @ 8-10 RM] superset with Dumbbell flyes [4 sets @ 8-10 RM] Low pulley row [4 sets @ 8-10 RM] Leg curl [4 sets @ 8-10 RM] Crunch [4 sets @ 15-20 RM]
Tuesday	Shoulders, Legs, Abdominals	Military press [4 sets @ 8-10 RM] triset with Lateral raises [4 sets @ 8-10 RM] e Rear lateral raises [4 sets @ 8-10 RM] Leg extension [4 sets @ 8-10 RM] superset with Leg Press [4 sets @ 8-10RM] Calf raise [4 sets @ 8-10 RM] Crunch [4 sets @ 15-20RM]
Wednesday	Arms, Abdominals	Dumbbell curl [4 sets @ 8-10RM] Cable pushdown [4 sets @ 8-10RM] Crunch [4 sets @ 15-20RM]
Thursday	Chest, Back, Legs, Abdominals	Dumbbell bench press [4 sets @ 8-10 RM] superset with Dumbbell flyes [4 sets @ 8-10 RM] Lat Machine [4 sets @ 8-10 RM] Leg curl [4 sets @ 8-10 RM] Crunch [4 sets @ 15-20 RM]
Friday	Shoulders, Legs, Abdominals	Military press [4 sets @ 8-10 RM] triset with Lateral raises [4 sets @ 8-10 RM] e Rear lateral raises [4 sets @ 8-10 RM] Leg extension [4 sets @ 8-10 RM] superset with Leg Press [4 sets @ 8-10RM] Calf raise [4 sets @ 8-10 RM] Crunch [4 sets @ 15-20RM]
Saturday	Rest	Aerobic Activity
Sunday	Rest	

[235]

=== Andrea Raimondi ===

Hypertrophy phase. Mesocycle 3. Week 10.
The number of series is increased with a medium-high load, rest of 60-90 " between the sets.

DAY	MUSCLES	EXERCICES
Monday	Chest, Back, Legs, Abdominals	Dumbbell bench press [5 sets @ 8-10 RM] superset with Dumbbell flyes [5 sets @ 8-10 RM] Low pulley row [5 sets @ 8-10 RM] Leg curl [5 sets @ 8-10 RM] Crunch [4 sets @ 15-20 RM]
Tuesday	Shoulders, Legs, Abdominals	Military press [5 sets @ 8-10 RM] triset with Lateral raises [5 sets @ 8-10 RM] e Rear lateral raises [5 sets @ 8-10 RM] Leg extension [5 sets @ 8-10 RM] superset Leg Press [4 sets @ 8-10RM] Calf raise [5 sets @ 8-10 RM] Crunch [4 sets @ 15-20RM]
Wednesday	Arms, Abdominals	Dumbbell curl [5 sets @ 8-10RM] Cable pushdown [5 sets @ 8-10RM] Crunch [4 sets @ 15-20RM]
Thursday	Chest, Back, Legs, Abdominals	Dumbbell bench press [5 sets @ 8-10 RM] superset with Dumbbell flyes [5 sets @ 8-10 RM] Lat Machine[5 sets @ 8-10 RM] Leg curl [5 sets @ 8-10 RM] Crunch [4 sets @ 15-20 RM]
Friday	Shoulders, Legs, Abdominals	Military press [5 sets @ 8-10 RM] triset with Lateral raises [5 sets @ 8-10 RM] e Rear lateral raises [5 sets @ 8-10 RM] Leg extension [5 sets @ 8-10 RM] superset with Leg Press [4 sets @ 8-10RM] Calf raise [5 sets @ 8-10 RM] Crunch [4 sets @ 15-20RM]
Saturday	Rest	Aerobic Activity
Sunday	Rest	

[236]

=== **Woman and Fitness** ===

Hypertrophy phase. Mesocycle 3. Week 11.
The loads are increased and become high to break homeostasis on the volume of work. Superset and triset techniques are introduced. Rest of 90-120 sets between sets

DAY	MUSCLES	EXERCICES
Monday	Chest, Back, Legs, Abdominals	Dumbbell bench press [4 sets @ 6-8 RM] superset with Dumbbell flyes [4 sets @ 6-8 RM] Low pulley row [4 sets @ 6-8 RM] Leg curl [4 sets @ 6-8 RM] Crunch [4 sets @ 15-20 RM]
Tuesday	Shoulders, Legs, Abdominals	Military press [4 sets @ 6-8 RM] triset with Lateral raises [4 sets @ 6-8 RM] e Rear lateral raises [4 sets @ 6-8 RM] Leg extension [4 sets @ 6-8 RM] superset with Leg Press [4 sets @ 6-8 RM] Calf raise [4 sets @ 6-8 RM] Crunch [4 sets @ 15-20RM]
Wednesday	Arms, Abdominals	Dumbbell curl [4 sets @ 6-8 RM] Cable pushdown [4 sets @ 6-8 RM] Crunch [4 sets @ 15-20RM]
Thursday	Chest, Back, Legs, Abdominals	Dumbbell bench press [4 sets @ 6-8 RM] superset with Dumbbell flyes [4 sets @ 6-8 RM] Lat Machine [4 sets @ 6-8 RM] Leg curl [4 sets @ 6-8 RM] Crunch [4 sets @ 15-20 RM]
Friday	Shoulders, Legs, Abdominals	Military press [4 sets @ 6-8 RM] triset with Lateral raises [4 sets @ 6-8 RM] e Rear lateral raises [4 sets @ 6-8 RM] Leg extension [4 sets @ 6-8 RM] superset with Leg Press [4 sets @ 6-8 RM] Calf raise [4 sets @ 6-8 RM] Crunch [4 sets @ 15-20RM]
Saturday	Rest	Aerobic Activity
Sunday	Rest	

Hypertrophy phase. Mesocycle 3. Week 12.
Week of weight unloading. Rest between the series of 60-90 secs.

DAY	MUSCLES	EXERCICES
Monday	Chest, Back, Legs, Abdominals	Dumbbell bench press [4 sets @ 15-20RM] Dumbbell flyes [4 sets @ 15-20RM] Low pulley row [4 sets @ 15-20RM] Leg curl [4 sets @ 15-20RM] Crunch [4 sets @ 15-20RM]
Tuesday	Shoulders, Legs, Abdominals	Military press [4 sets @ 15-20RM] Lateral raises [4 sets @ 15-20RM] Rear lateral raises [4 sets @ 15-20RM] Leg extension [4 sets @ 15-20RM] Leg Press [4 sets @ 15-20RM] Calf raise [4 sets @ 15-20RM] Crunch [4 sets @ 15-20RM]
Wednesday	Arms, Abdominals	Dumbbell curl [3 sets @ 15-20RM] Cable pushdown [3 sets @ 15-20RM] Crunch [4 sets @ 15-20RM]
Thursday	Chest, Back, Legs, Abdominals	Dumbbell bench press [4 sets @ 15-20RM] Dumbbell flyes [4 sets @ 15-20RM] Lat Machine [4 sets @ 15-20RM] Leg curl [4 sets @ 15-20RM] Crunch [4 sets @ 15-20RM]
Friday	Shoulders, Legs, Abdominals	Military press [4 sets @ 15-20RM] Lateral raises [4 sets @ 15-20RM] Rear lateral raises [4 sets @ 15-20RM] Leg extension [4 sets @ 15-20RM] Leg Press [4 sets @ 15-20RM] Calf raise [4 sets @ 15-20RM] Crunch [4 sets @ 15-20RM]
Saturday	Rest	Aerobic Activity
Sunday	Rest	

=== The Shape Of Body To Come ===

After 12 weeks of the hypertrophy protocol, we can verify our state of form concerning the desired goals, we then can continue with the metabolic adaptation protocol for a four-week Mesocycle. These four weeks can lead to an increase in muscle definition when done at high rates and with a calorie deficit. Or we can decide to stop training for 2-3 weeks and then start again with a phase of strength or hypertrophy. This stop period could coincide with the summer holidays in which you reach the maximum of muscle development and your condition.

Strength Phase #2

If you have the goal of increasing strength, you can proceed with a second phase for strength. In this new period, some exercises can be changed, the important thing is to gradually increase the loads, following the proposed progression, week after week. At this stage, it is advisable to train more the muscles less strong.

=== Woman and Fitness ===

Strength Phase # 2. Section 1. Week 1
Perceived Effort Level 8, Increase Loads With Each Set.

DAY	MUSCLES	EXERCICES
Monday	Full Body	Bench press [3 sets @ 5-6 RM] Military press [3 sets @ 5-6 RM] Low pulley row [3 sets @ 5-6 RM] Dumbbell curl [3 sets @ 5-6 RM] Cable pushdown [3 sets @ 5-6 RM] Leg curl [3 sets @ 5-6 RM] Squat [3 sets @ 5-6 RM] Crunch [3 sets @ 15-20RM]
Tuesday	Rest	
Wednesday	Full Body	Bench press [3 sets @ 5-6 RM] Military press [3 sets @ 5-6 RM] Low pulley row [3 sets @ 5-6 RM] Dumbbell curl [3 sets @ 5-6 RM] Cable pushdown [3 sets @ 5-6 RM] Leg curl [3 sets @ 5-6 RM] Squat [3 sets @ 5-6 RM] Crunch [3 sets @ 15-20RM]
Thursday	Rest	
Friday	Full Body	Bench press [3 sets @ 5-6 RM] Military press [3 sets @ 5-6 RM] Low pulley row [3 sets @ 5-6 RM] Dumbbell curl [3 sets @ 5-6 RM] Cable pushdown [3 sets @ 5-6 RM] Leg curl [3 sets @ 5-6 RM] Squat [3 sets @ 5-6 RM] Crunch [3 sets @ 15-20RM]
Saturday	Rest	Aerobic Activity
Sunday	Rest	

[241]

Strength Phase # 2. Section 1. Week 2
Perceived Effort Level 8, Increase Loads With Each Set.

DAY	MUSCLES	EXERCICES
Monday	Full Body	Bench press [3 sets @ 3-5 RM] Military press [3 sets @ 3-5 RM] Low pulley row [3 sets @ 3-5 RM] Dumbbell curl [3 sets @ 3-5 RM] Cable pushdown [3 sets @ 3-5 RM] Leg curl [3 sets @ 3-5 RM] Squat [3 sets @ 3-5 RM] Crunch [3 sets @ 15-20RM]
Tuesday	Rest	
Wednesd ay	Full Body	Bench press [3 sets @ 3-5 RM] Military press [3 sets @ 3-5 RM] Low pulley row [3 sets @ 3-5 RM] Dumbbell curl [3 sets @ 3-5 RM] Cable pushdown [3 sets @ 3-5 RM] Leg curl [3 sets @ 3-5 RM] Squat [3 sets @ 3-5 RM] Crunch [3 sets @ 15-20RM]
Thursday	Rest	
Friday	Full Body	Bench press [3 sets @ 3-5 RM] Military press [3 sets @ 3-5 RM] Low pulley row [3 sets @ 3-5 RM] Dumbbell curl [3 sets @ 3-5 RM] Cable pushdown [3 sets @ 3-5 RM] Leg curl [3 sets @ 3-5 RM] Squat [3 sets @ 3-5 RM] Crunch [3 sets @ 15-20RM]
Saturday	Rest	Aerobic Activity
Sunday	Rest	

=== **Woman and Fitness** ===

Strength Phase # 2. Section 1. Week 3
Perceived Effort Level 8, Increase Loads With Each Set.

DAY	MUSCLES	EXERCICES
Monday	Full Body	Bench press [3 sets @ 1-3 RM] Military press [3 sets @ 1-3 RM] Low pulley row [3 sets @ 1-3 RM] Dumbbell curl [3 sets @ 1-3 RM] Cable pushdown [3 sets @ 1-3 RM] Leg curl [3 sets @ 1-3 RM] Squat [3 sets @ 1-3 RM] Crunch [3 sets @ 15-20RM]
Tuesday	Rest	
Wednesday	Full Body	Bench press [3 sets @ 1-3 RM] Military press [3 sets @ 1-3 RM] Low pulley row [3 sets @ 1-3 RM] Dumbbell curl [3 sets @ 1-3 RM] Cable pushdown [3 sets @ 1-3 RM] Leg curl [3 sets @ 1-3 RM] Squat [3 sets @ 1-3 RM] Crunch [3 sets @ 15-20RM]
Thursday	Rest	
Friday	Full Body	Bench press [3 sets @ 1-3 RM] Military press [3 sets @ 1-3 RM] Low pulley row [3 sets @ 1-3 RM] Dumbbell curl [3 sets @ 1-3 RM] Cable pushdown [3 sets @ 1-3 RM] Leg curl [3 sets @ 1-3 RM] Squat [3 sets @ 1-3 RM] Crunch [3 sets @ 15-20RM]
Saturday	Rest	Aerobic Activity
Sunday	Rest	

Strength Phase # 2. Section 1. Week 4
Perceived Effort Level 7.

DAY	MUSCLES	EXERCICES
Monday	Full Body	Bench press [3 sets @ 10-12 RM] Military press [3 sets @ 10-12 RM] Low pulley row [3 sets @ 10-12 RM] Dumbbell curl [3 sets @ 10-12 RM] Cable pushdown [3 sets @ 10-12 RM] Leg curl [3 sets @ 10-12 RM] Squat [3 sets @ 10-12 RM] Crunch [3 sets @ 15-20RM]
Tuesday	Rest	
Wednesday	Full Body	Bench press [3 sets @ 10-12 RM] Military press [3 sets @ 10-12 RM] Low pulley row [3 sets @ 10-12 RM] Dumbbell curl [3 sets @ 10-12 RM] Cable pushdown [3 sets @ 10-12 RM] Leg curl [3 sets @ 10-12 RM] Squat [3 sets @ 10-12 RM] Crunch [3 sets @ 15-20RM]
Thursday	Rest	
Friday	Full Body	Bench press [3 sets @ 10-12 RM] Military press [3 sets @ 10-12 RM] Low pulley row [3 sets @ 10-12 RM] Dumbbell curl [3 sets @ 10-12 RM] Cable pushdown [3 sets @ 10-12 RM] Leg curl [3 sets @ 10-12 RM] Squat [3 sets @ 10-12 RM] Crunch [3 sets @ 15-20RM]
Saturday	Rest	Aerobic Activity
Sunday	Rest	

=== Woman and Fitness ===

Strength Phase # 2. Section 2. Week 5
Perceived Effort Level 8, Increase Loads With Each Set.

DAY	MUSCLES	EXERCICES
Monday	Upper Body	Bench press [3 sets @ 6-8 RM] Military press [3 sets @ 6-8 RM] Dumbbell flyes [3 sets @ 6-8 RM] Lat machine [3 sets @ 6-8 RM] Dumbbell curl [3 sets @ 6-8 RM] Cable pushdown [3 sets @ 6-8 RM]
Tuesday	Lower Body	Leg curl [3 sets @ 6-8 RM] Squat [3 sets @ 6-8 RM] Calf raise [3 sets @ 6-8 RM] Crunch [3 sets @ 15-20RM]
Wednesday	Rest	
Thursday	Upper Body	Bench press [3 sets @ 6-8 RM] Military press [3 sets @ 6-8 RM] Lateral raises[3 sets @ 6-8 RM] Lat machine [3 sets @ 6-8 RM] Dumbbell curl [3 sets @ 6-8 RM] Cable pushdown [3 sets @ 6-8 RM]
Friday	Lower Body	Leg curl [3 sets @ 6-8 RM] Squat [3 sets @ 6-8 RM] Calf raise [3 sets @ 6-8 RM] Crunch [3 sets @ 15-20RM]
Saturday	Rest	Aerobic Activity
Sunday	Rest	

Strength Phase # 2. Section 2. Week 6
Perceived Effort Level 8, Increase Loads With Each Set.

DAY	MUSCLES	EXERCICES
Monday	Upper Body	Bench press [3 sets @ 3-5 RM] Military press [3 sets @ 3-5 RM] Dumbbell flyes [3 sets @ 3-5 RM] Lat machine [3 sets @ 3-5 RM] Dumbbell curl [3 sets @ 3-5 RM] Cable pushdown [3 sets @ 3-5 RM]
Tuesday	Lower Body	Leg curl [3 sets @ 3-5 RM] Squat [3 sets @ 3-5 RM] Calf raise [3 sets @ 3-5 RM] Crunch [3 sets @ 15-20RM]
Wednesday	Rest	
Thursday	Upper Body	Bench press [3 sets @ 3-5 RM] Military press [3 sets @ 3-5 RM] Lateral raises[3 sets @3-5 RM] Lat machine [3 sets @ 3-5 RM] Dumbbell curl [3 sets @ 3-5 RM] Cable pushdown [3 sets @ 3-5 RM]
Friday	Lower Body	Leg curl [3 sets @ 3-5 RM] Squat [3 sets @ 3-5 RM] Calf raise [3 sets @ 3-5 RM] Crunch [3 sets @ 15-20RM]
Saturday	Rest	Aerobic Activity
Sunday	Rest	

=== **Woman and Fitness** ===

Strength Phase # 2. Section 2. Week 7
Perceived Effort Level 9, Increase Loads With Each Set.

DAY	MUSCLES	EXERCICES
Monday	Upper Body	Bench press [3 sets @ 2-3 RM] Military press [3 sets @ 2-3 RM] Dumbbell flyes [3 sets @ 2-3 RM] Lat machine [3 sets @ 2-3 RM] Dumbbell curl [3 sets @ 2-3 RM] Cable pushdown [3 sets @ 2-3 RM]
Tuesday	Lower Body	Leg curl [3 sets @ 2-3 RM] Squat [3 sets @ 2-3 RM] Calf raise [3 sets @ 2-3 RM] Crunch [3 sets @ 15-20RM]
Wednesday	Rest	
Thursday	Upper Body	Bench press [3 sets @ 2-3 RM] Military press [3 sets @ 2-3 RM] Lateral raises[3 sets @2-3 RM] Lat machine [3 sets @ 2-3 RM] Dumbbell curl [3 sets @ 2-3 RM] Cable pushdown [3 sets @ 2-3 RM]
Friday	Lower Body	Leg curl [3 sets @ 2-3 RM] Squat [3 sets @ 2-3 RM] Calf raise [3 sets @ 2-3 RM] Crunch [3 sets @ 15-20RM]
Saturday	Rest	Aerobic Activity
Sunday	Rest	

[247]

Strength Phase # 2. Section 2. Week 8
Perceived Effort Level 7, Increase Loads With Each Set.

DAY	MUSCLES	EXERCICES
Monday	Upper Body	Bench press [3 sets @ 10-12 RM] Military press [3 sets @ 10-12 RM] Dumbbell flyes [3 sets @ 10-12RM] Lat machine [3 sets @ 10-12 RM] Dumbbell curl [3 sets @ 10-12 RM] Cable pushdown [3 sets @ 10-12 RM]
Tuesday	Lower Body	Leg curl [3 sets @ 10-12 RM] Squat [3 sets @ 10-12 RM] Calf raise [3 sets @ 10-12 RM] Crunch [3 sets @ 15-20RM]
Wednesday	Rest	
Thursday	Upper Body	Bench press [3 sets @ 10-12 RM] Military press [3 sets @ 10-12 RM] Dumbbell flyes [3 sets @ 10-12 RM] Lat machine [3 sets @ 10-12 RM] Dumbbell curl [3 sets @ 10-12 RM] Cable pushdown [3 sets @ 10-12 RM]
Friday	Lower Body	Leg curl [3 sets @ 10-12 RM] Squat [3 sets @ 10-12 RM] Calf raise [3 sets @ 10-12 RM] Crunch [3 sets @ 15-20RM]
Saturday	Rest	Aerobic Activity
Sunday	Rest	

=== The Shape Of Body To Come ===

Hypertrophy Phase #2

If you have an annual goal of muscle mass gain, you can proceed with a new phase of hypertrophy. In this new phase, it is possible to modify some exercises performed, always following the proposed progression. You must also evaluate your fitness state: if you think, for example, that the muscles of the legs are not as you would like, it is good to increase the exercises for the Legs, or you want to increase the muscles of the arms more, perform more exercises for that group muscular. At this point in the program you should be stronger than the first phase, so use more weight in each exercise.

=== Andrea Raimondi ===

Hypertrophy Phase #2. Mesocycle 1. Week 1.

DAY	MUSCLES	EXERCICES
Monday	Full Body	Dumbbell bench press[3 sets @ 10-12RM] Dumbbell military press [3 sets @ 10-12RM] Low pulley row [3 sets @ 10-12RM] Dumbbell curl [3 sets @ 10-12RM] Cable pushdown [3 sets @ 10-12RM] Leg curl [3 sets @ 10-12RM] Leg extension [3 sets @ 10-12RM] Crunch [3 sets @ 10-12RM] Calf raise [3 sets @ 10-12RM]
Tuesday	Rest	
Wednesday	Full Body	Dumbbell flyes [3 sets @ 10-12RM] Lateral raises[3 sets @ 10-12RM] Lat machine [3 sets @ 10-12RM] Dumbbell curl [3 sets @ 10-12RM] Cable pushdown [3 sets @ 10-12RM] Leg curl [3 sets @ 10-12RM] Leg extension [3 sets @ 10-12RM] Crunch [3 sets @ 10-12RM] Calf raise [3 sets @ 10-12RM]
Thursday	Rest	
Friday	Full Body	Dumbbell bench press[3 sets @ 10-12RM] Dumbbell military press [3 sets @ 10-12RM] Low pulley row [3 sets @ 10-12RM] Dumbbell curl [3 sets @ 10-12RM] Cable pushdown [3 sets @ 10-12RM] Leg curl [3 sets @ 10-12RM] Leg extension [3 sets @ 10-12RM] Crunch [3 sets @ 10-12RM] Calf raise [3 sets @ 10-12RM]
Saturday	Rest	Aerobic Activity
Sunday	Rest	

=== **Woman and Fitness** ===

Hypertrophy Phase #2. Mesocycle 1. Week 2.

DAY	MUSCLES	EXERCICES
Monday	Full Body	Dumbbell bench press[3 sets @ 8-10RM] Dumbbell military press [3 sets @ 1 8-10RM] Low pulley row [3 sets @ 8-10RM] Dumbbell curl [3 sets @ 8-10RM] Cable pushdown [3 sets @ 8-10RM] Leg curl [3 sets @ 8-10RM] Leg extension [3 sets @ 8-10RM] Crunch [3 sets @ 8-10RM] Calf raise [3 sets @ 8-10RM]
Tuesday	Rest	
Wednesday	Full Body	Dumbbell flyes [3 sets @ 8-10RM] Lateral raises[3 sets @ 8-10RM] Lat machine [3 sets @ 8-10RM] Dumbbell curl [3 sets @ 8-10RM] Cable pushdown [3 sets @ 8-10RM] Leg curl [3 sets @ 8-10RM] Leg extension [3 sets @ 8-10RM] Crunch [3 sets @ 8-10RM] Calf raise [3 sets @ 8-10RM]
Thursday	Rest	
Friday	Full Body	Dumbbell bench press[3 sets @ 8-10RM] Dumbbell military press [3 sets @ 1 8-10RM] Low pulley row [3 sets @ 8-10RM] Dumbbell curl [3 sets @ 8-10RM] Cable pushdown [3 sets @ 8-10RM] Leg curl [3 sets @ 8-10RM] Leg extension [3 sets @ 8-10RM] Crunch [3 sets @ 8-10RM] Calf raise [3 sets @ 8-10RM]
Saturday	Rest	
Sunday	Rest	

Hypertrophy Phase #2. Mesocycle 1. Week 3.

Increase the loads and reduce the repetitions, always keeping maximum control of the execution. 60-sec recovery between one set and the other.

DAY	MUSCLES	EXERCICES
Monday	Full Body	Dumbbell bench press[3 sets @ 6-8RM] Dumbbell military press [3 sets @ 6-8RM] Low pulley row [3 sets @ 6-8RM] Dumbbell curl [3 sets @ 6-8 RM] Cable pushdown [3 sets @ 6-8RM] Leg curl [3 sets @ 6-8RM] Leg extension [3 sets @ 6-8RM] Crunch [3 sets @ 6-8RM] Calf raise [3 sets @ 6-8RM]
Tuesday	Rest	
Wednesday	Full Body	Dumbbell flyes [3 sets @ 6-8RM] Lateral raises[3 sets @ 6-8RM] Lat machine [3 sets @ 6-8RM] Dumbbell curl [3 sets @ 6-8RM] Cable pushdown [3 sets @ 6-8RM] Leg curl [3 sets @ 6-8RM] Leg extension [3 sets @ 6-8RM] Crunch [3 sets @ 6-8RM] Calf raise [3 sets @ 6-8RM]
Thursday	Rest	
Friday	Full Body	Dumbbell bench press[3 sets @ 6-8RM] Dumbbell military press [3 sets @ 6-8RM] Low pulley row [3 sets @ 6-8RM] Dumbbell curl [3 sets @ 6-8 RM] Cable pushdown [3 sets @ 6-8RM] Leg curl [3 sets @ 6-8RM] Leg extension [3 sets @ 6-8RM] Crunch [3 sets @ 6-8RM] Calf raise [3 sets @ 6-8RM]
Saturday	Rest	Aerobic Activity
Sunday	Rest	

=== Woman and Fitness ===

Hypertrophy Phase #2. Mesocycle 1. Week 4.
Decrease loads and increase repetitions, recovery 45-60sec.

DAY	MUSCLES	EXERCICES
Monday	Full Body	Dumbbell bench press[3 sets @ 10-12RM] Dumbbell military press [3 sets @ 10-12RM] Low pulley row [3 sets @ 10-12RM] Dumbbell curl [3 sets @ 10-12RM] Cable pushdown [3 sets @ 10-12RM] Leg curl [3 sets @ 10-12RM] Leg extension [3 sets @ 10-12RM] Crunch [3 sets @ 10-12RM] Calf raise [3 sets @ 10-12RM]
Tuesday	Rest	
Wednesday	Full Body	Dumbbell flyes [3 sets @ 10-12RM] Lateral raises[3 sets @ 10-12RM] Lat machine [3 sets @ 10-12RM] Dumbbell curl [3 sets @ 10-12RM] Cable pushdown [3 sets @ 10-12RM] Leg curl [3 sets @ 10-12RM] Leg extension [3 sets @ 10-12RM] Crunch [3 sets @ 10-12RM] Calf raise [3 sets @ 10-12RM]
Thursday	Rest	
Friday	Full Body	Dumbbell bench press[3 sets @ 10-12RM] Dumbbell military press [3 sets @ 10-12RM] Low pulley row [3 sets @ 10-12RM] Dumbbell curl [3 sets @ 10-12RM] Cable pushdown [3 sets @ 10-12RM] Leg curl [3 sets @ 10-12RM] Leg extension [3 sets @ 10-12RM] Crunch [3 sets @ 10-12RM] Calf raise [3 sets @ 10-12RM]
Saturday	Rest	Aerobic Activity
Sunday	Rest	

[253]

Hypertrophy Phase #2. Mesocycle 2. Week 5.

DAY	MUSCLES	EXERCICES
Monday	Chest, Back, Legs, Abdominals	Dumbbell bench press[4 sets @ 10-12RM] Dumbbell flyes [4 sets @ 10-12RM] Low pulley row [4 sets @ 10-12RM] Leg curl [4 sets @ 10-12RM] Crunch [4 sets @ 10-12RM]
Tuesday	Shoulders, Legs, Abdominals	Military press [4 sets @ 10-12RM] Lateral raises [4 sets @ 10-12RM] Rear lateral raises [4 sets @ 10-12RM] Leg extension [4 sets @ 10-12RM] Leg Press [4 sets @ 10-12RM] Calf raise [4 sets @ 10-12RM] Crunch [4 sets @ 10-12RM]
Wednesday	Arms, Abdominals	Dumbbell curl [3 sets @ 10-12RM] Cable pushdown [3 sets @ 10-12RM] Crunch [4 sets @ 10-12RM]
Thursday	Chest, Back, Legs, Abdominals	Dumbbell bench press[4 sets @ 10-12RM] Dumbbell flyes [4 sets @ 10-12RM] Lat machine [4 sets @ 10-12RM] Leg curl [4 sets @ 10-12RM] Crunch [4 sets @ 10-12RM]
Friday	Shoulders, Legs, Abdominals	Military press [4 sets @ 10-12RM] Lateral raises [4 sets @ 10-12RM] Rear lateral raises [4 sets @ 10-12RM] Leg extension [4 sets @ 10-12RM] Leg Press [4 sets @ 10-12RM] Calf raise [4 sets @ 10-12RM] Crunch [4 sets @ 10-12RM]
Saturday	Rest	Aerobic Activity
Sunday	Rest	

=== Woman and Fitness ===

Hypertrophy Phase #2. Mesocycle 2. Week 6.
Increase loads, 60-90 sec recovery.

DAY	MUSCLES	EXERCICES
Monday	Chest, Back, Legs, Abdominals	Dumbbell bench press[4 sets @ 8-10RM] Dumbbell flyes [4 sets @ 8-10RM] Low pulley row [4 sets @ 8-10RM] Leg curl [4 sets @ 8-10RM] Crunch [4 sets @ 15-20RM]
Tuesday	Shoulders, Legs, Abdominals	Military press [4 sets @ 8-10RM] Lateral raises [4 sets @ 8-10RM] Rear lateral raises [4 sets @ 8-10RM] Leg extension [4 sets @ 8-10RM] Leg Press [4 sets @ 8-10RM] Calf raise [4 sets @ 8-10RM] Crunch [4 sets @ 15-20RM]
Wednesday	Arms, Abdominals	Dumbbell curl [4 sets @ 8-10RM] Cable pushdown [4 sets @ 8-10RM] Crunch [4 sets @ 8-10RM]
Thursday	Chest, Back, Legs, Abdominals	Dumbbell bench press[4 sets @ 8-10RM] Dumbbell flyes [4 sets @ 8-10RM] Lat machine [4 sets @ 8-10RM] Leg curl [4 sets @ 8-10RM] Crunch [4 sets @ 15-20RM]
Friday	Shoulders, Legs, Abdominals	Military press [4 sets @ 8-10RM] Lateral raises [4 sets @ 8-10RM] Rear lateral raises [4 sets @ 8-10RM] Leg extension [4 sets @ 8-10RM] Leg Press [4 sets @ 8-10RM] Calf raise [4 sets @ 8-10RM] Crunch [4 sets @ 15-20RM]
Saturday	Rest	Aerobic Activity
Sunday	Rest	

Hypertrophy Phase #2. Mesocycle 2. Week 7.

Increase loads, use heavy loads, recovery 60-90 sec.

DAY	MUSCLES	EXERCICES
Monday	Chest, Back, Legs, Abdominals	Dumbbell bench press[5 sets @ 8-10 RM] Dumbbell flyes [5 sets @ 8-10 RM] Low pulley row [5 sets @ 8-10 RM] Leg curl [5 sets @ 8-10 RM] Crunch [4 sets @ 15-20 RM]
Tuesday	Shoulders, Legs, Abdominals	Military press [5 sets @ 8-10 RM] Lateral raises [5 sets @ 8-10 RM] Rear lateral raises [5 sets @ 8-10 RM] Leg extension [5 sets @ 8-10 RM] Leg Press [4 sets @ 8-10RM] Calf raise [5 sets @ 8-10 RM] Crunch [4 sets @ 15-20RM]
Wednesday	Arms, Abdominals	Dumbbell curl [5 sets @ 8-10RM] Cable pushdown [5 sets @ 8-10RM] Crunch [4 sets @ 15-20RM]
Thursday	Chest, Back, Legs, Abdominals	Dumbbell bench press[5 sets @ 8-10 RM] Dumbbell flyes [5 sets @ 8-10 RM] Lat machine [5 sets @ 8-10 RM] Leg curl [5 sets @ 8-10 RM] Crunch [4 sets @ 15-20 RM]
Friday	Shoulders, Legs, Abdominals	Military press [5 sets @ 8-10 RM] Lateral raises [5 sets @ 8-10 RM] Rear lateral raises [5 sets @ 8-10 RM] Leg extension [5 sets @ 8-10 RM] Leg Press [4 sets @ 8-10RM] Calf raise [5 sets @ 8-10 RM] Crunch [4 sets @ 15-20RM]
Saturday	Rest	Aerobic Activity
Sunday	Rest	

=== Woman and Fitness ===

Hypertrophy Phase #2. Mesocycle 2. Week 8.

Increase loads, use heavy loads, recovery 60-90 sec.

DAY	MUSCLES	EXERCICES
Monday	Chest, Back, Legs, Abdominals	Dumbbell bench press[4 sets @ 15-20RM] Dumbbell flyes [4 sets @ 15-20RM] Low pulley row [4 sets @ 15-20RM] Leg curl [4 sets @ 15-20RM] Crunch [4 sets @ 15-20RM]
Tuesday	Shoulders, Legs, Abdominals	Military press [4 sets @ 15-20RM] Lateral raises [4 sets @ 15-20RM] Rear lateral raises [4 sets @ 15-20RM] Leg extension [4 sets @ 15-20RM] Leg Press [4 sets @ 15-20RM] Calf raise [4 sets @ 15-20RM] Crunch [4 sets @ 15-20RM]
Wednesday	Arms, Abdominals	Dumbbell curl [3 sets @ 15-20RM] Cable pushdown [3 sets @ 15-20RM] Crunch [4 sets @ 15-20RM]
Thursday	Chest, Back, Legs, Abdominals	Dumbbell bench press[4 sets @ 15-20RM] Dumbbell flyes [4 sets @ 15-20RM] Lat machine [4 sets @ 15-20RM] Leg curl [4 sets @ 15-20RM] Crunch [4 sets @ 15-20RM]
Friday	Shoulders, Legs, Abdominals	Military press [4 sets @ 15-20RM] Lateral raises [4 sets @ 15-20RM] Rear lateral raises [4 sets @ 15-20RM] Leg extension [4 sets @ 15-20RM] Leg Press [4 sets @ 15-20RM] Calf raise [4 sets @ 15-20RM] Crunch [4 sets @ 15-20RM]
Saturday	Rest	Aerobic Activity
Sunday	Rest	

=== Andrea Raimondi ===

Hypertrophy Phase #2. Mesocycle 3. Week 9.
Superset e triset. Rest 60-90 secs

DAY	MUSCLES	EXERCICES
Monday	Chest, Back, Legs, Abdominals	Dumbbell bench press[4 sets @ 8-10 RM] superset with Dumbbell flyes [4 sets @ 8-10 RM] Low pulley row [4 sets @ 8-10 RM] Leg curl [4 sets @ 8-10 RM] Crunch [4 sets @ 15-20 RM]
Tuesday	Shoulders, Legs, Abdominals	Military press [4 sets @ 8-10 RM] triset with Lateral raises [4 sets @ 8-10 RM] e Rear lateral raises [4 sets @ 8-10 RM] Leg extension [4 sets @ 8-10 RM] superset with Leg Press [4 sets @ 8-10RM] Calf raise [4 sets @ 8-10 RM] Crunch [4 sets @ 15-20RM]
Wednesday	Arms, Abdominals	Dumbbell curl [4 sets @ 8-10RM] Cable pushdown [4 sets @ 8-10RM] Crunch [4 sets @ 15-20RM]
Thursday	Chest, Back, Legs, Abdominals	Dumbbell bench press[4 sets @ 8-10 RM] superset with Dumbbell flyes [4 sets @ 8-10 RM] Lat machine [4 sets @ 8-10 RM] Leg curl [4 sets @ 8-10 RM] Crunch [4 sets @ 15-20 RM]
Friday	Shoulders, Legs, Abdominals	Military press [4 sets @ 8-10 RM] triset with Lateral raises [4 sets @ 8-10 RM] e Rear lateral raises [4 sets @ 8-10 RM] Leg extension [4 sets @ 8-10 RM] superset with Leg Press [4 sets @ 8-10RM] Calf raise [4 sets @ 8-10 RM] Crunch [4 sets @ 15-20RM]
Saturday	Rest	Aerobic Activity
Sunday	Rest	

=== Woman and Fitness ===

Hypertrophy Phase #2. Mesocycle 3. Week 10.

DAY	MUSCLES	EXERCICES
Monday	Chest, Back, Legs, Abdominals	Dumbbell bench press[5 sets @ 8-10 RM] superset with Dumbbell flyes [5 sets @ 8-10 RM] Low pulley row [5 sets @ 8-10 RM] Leg curl [5 sets @ 8-10 RM] Crunch [4 sets @ 15-20 RM]
Tuesday	Shoulders, Legs, Abdominals	Military press [5 sets @ 8-10 RM] triset with Lateral raises [5 sets @ 8-10 RM] e Rear lateral raises [5 sets @ 8-10 RM] Leg extension [5 sets @ 8-10 RM] superset Leg Press [4 sets @ 8-10RM] Calf raise [5 sets @ 8-10 RM] Crunch [4 sets @ 15-20RM]
Wednesday	Arms, Abdominals	Dumbbell curl [5 sets @ 8-10RM] Cable pushdown [5 sets @ 8-10RM] Crunch [4 sets @ 15-20RM]
Thursday	Chest, Back, Legs, Abdominals	Dumbbell bench press[5 sets @ 8-10 RM] superset with Dumbbell flyes [5 sets @ 8-10 RM] Lat machine[5 sets @ 8-10 RM] Leg curl [5 sets @ 8-10 RM] Crunch [4 sets @ 15-20 RM]
Friday	Shoulders, Legs, Abdominals	Military press [5 sets @ 8-10 RM] triset with Lateral raises [5 sets @ 8-10 RM] e Rear lateral raises [5 sets @ 8-10 RM] Leg extension [5 sets @ 8-10 RM] superset with Leg Press [4 sets @ 8-10RM] Calf raise [5 sets @ 8-10 RM] Crunch [4 sets @ 15-20RM]
Saturday	Rest	Aerobic Activity
Sunday	Rest	

Hypertrophy Phase #2. Mesocycle 3. Week 11.
Increase loads. Rest 90-120 sec.

DAY	MUSCLES	EXERCICES
Monday	Chest, Back, Legs, Abdominals	Dumbbell bench press[4 sets @ 6-8 RM] superset with Dumbbell flyes [4 sets @ 6-8 RM] Low pulley row [4 sets @ 6-8 RM] Leg curl [4 sets @ 6-8 RM] Crunch [4 sets @ 15-20 RM]
Tuesday	Shoulders, Legs, Abdominals	Military press [4 sets @ 6-8 RM] triset with Lateral raises [4 sets @ 6-8 RM] e Rear lateral raises [4 sets @ 6-8 RM] Leg extension [4 sets @ 6-8 RM] superset with Leg Press [4 sets @ 6-8 RM] Calf raise [4 sets @ 6-8 RM] Crunch [4 sets @ 15-20RM]
Wednesday	Arms, Abdominals	Dumbbell curl [4 sets @ 6-8 RM] Cable pushdown [4 sets @ 6-8 RM] Crunch [4 sets @ 15-20RM]
Thursday	Chest, Back, Legs, Abdominals	Dumbbell bench press[4 sets @ 6-8 RM] superset with Dumbbell flyes [4 sets @ 6-8 RM] Lat machine [4 sets @ 6-8 RM] Leg curl [4 sets @ 6-8 RM] Crunch [4 sets @ 15-20 RM]
Friday	Shoulders, Legs, Abdominals	Military press [4 sets @ 6-8 RM] triset with Lateral raises [4 sets @ 6-8 RM] e Rear lateral raises [4 sets @ 6-8 RM] Leg extension [4 sets @ 6-8 RM] superset with Leg Press [4 sets @ 6-8 RM] Calf raise [4 sets @ 6-8 RM] Crunch [4 sets @ 15-20RM]
Saturday	Rest	Aerobic Activity
Sunday	Rest	

=== Woman and Fitness ===

Hypertrophy Phase #2. Mesocycle 3. Week 12.
Increase loads. Rest 90-120 sec.

DAY	MUSCLES	EXERCICES
Monday	Chest, Back, Legs, Abdominals	Dumbbell bench press[4 sets @ 15-20RM] Dumbbell flyes [4 sets @ 15-20RM] Low pulley row [4 sets @ 15-20RM] Leg curl [4 sets @ 15-20RM] Crunch [4 sets @ 15-20RM]
Tuesday	Shoulders, Legs, Abdominals	Military press [4 sets @ 15-20RM] Lateral raises [4 sets @ 15-20RM] Rear lateral raises [4 sets @ 15-20RM] Leg extension [4 sets @ 15-20RM] Leg Press [4 sets @ 15-20RM] Calf raise [4 sets @ 15-20RM] Crunch [4 sets @ 15-20RM]
Wednesday	Arms, Abdominals	Dumbbell curl [3 sets @ 15-20RM] Cable pushdown [3 sets @ 15-20RM] Crunch [4 sets @ 15-20RM]
Thursday	Chest, Back, Legs, Abdominals	Dumbbell bench press[4 sets @ 15-20RM] Dumbbell flyes [4 sets @ 15-20RM] Lat machine [4 sets @ 15-20RM] Leg curl [4 sets @ 15-20RM] Crunch [4 sets @ 15-20RM]
Friday	Shoulders, Legs, Abdominals	Military press [4 sets @ 15-20RM] Lateral raises [4 sets @ 15-20RM] Rear lateral raises [4 sets @ 15-20RM] Leg extension [4 sets @ 15-20RM] Leg Press [4 sets @ 15-20RM] Calf raise [4 sets @ 15-20RM] Crunch [4 sets @ 15-20RM]
Saturday	Rest	Aerobic Activity
Sunday	Rest	

Leg metabolism activation

Below I have included three training programs for the metabolic activation of the lower body area, with exercises for the legs and buttocks. This program is to be performed on days of rest from the usual workouts, or as a real workout in its own right, or it can replace the exercises related to the legs in the weekly training sessions.

Program 1 / DAY 1

Hip Thrust	5 minutes
Step up	15 minutes
Dumbbell Squat	50 reps

Program 2 / DAY 2

Hip Thrust	25 reps
Step up	5 minutes
Dumbbell Squat	20 reps
Hip Thrust	25 reps
Dumbbell Squat	20 reps

Program 3 / DAY 3

Hip Thrust	5 minutes
Affondi in camminata	15 minutes
Dumbbell Squat	50 reps

=== Woman and Fitness ===

Lunch Break Training

Usually, women have to manage many responsibilities between family and work, and time for training is among the last things to do.

In these pages, I propose a workout to be carried out during the lunch break every working day.

It is a short workout, about 35-40 minutes. Following the principles of the progression of loads, as I indicated in the workouts of the various phases that you have read in the previous pages and keeping the recoveries under one minute, can give great results.

In the example week that I propose you will train the chest and shoulders 2 times a week, the legs 5 times, and the back 4 times.

Modify the number of exercises in each muscle district according to your needs: you can decide, for example, to train your chest or shoulders more and less your back and legs.

This workout can be used for at least three months, without being hurried to see the results, it takes time, as in all aspects concerning changes in a person's physique.

[263]

Example of a weekly lunch break training plan

DAY	MUSCLES	EXERCICES
Monday	Chest, Back, Legs, Abdominals	Dumbbell bench press[4 sets @ 12RM] Low pulley row [4 sets @ 12RM] Leg extension [4 sets @ 12RM] Crunch [2 sets @ 30 reps]
Tuesday	Shoulders, Legs, Back, Abdominals	Military press [4 sets @ 12RM] Lateral raises [4 sets @ 12RM] Lat Machine [4 sets @ 12RM] Leg curl [4 sets @ 12RM] Crunch [4 sets @ 30 reps]
Wednesday	Arms, Legs, Abdominals	Dumbbell curl [4 sets @ 12RM] Cable pushdown [4 sets @ 12RM] Leg Press [4 sets @ 20 RM] Crunch [4 sets @ 15-20RM]
Thursday	Chest, Back, Legs, Abdominals	Dumbbell bench press[4 sets @ 12RM] Low pulley row [4 sets @ 12RM] Leg extension [4 sets @ 12RM] Crunch [2 sets @ 30 reps]
Friday	Shoulders, Legs, Back, Abdominals	Military press [4 sets @ 12RM] Lateral raises [4 sets @ 12RM] Lat Machine [4 sets @ 12RM] Leg curl [4 sets @ 12RM] Crunch [4 sets @ 30 reps]
Saturday	Rest	Aerobic Activity
Sunday	Rest	

=== Woman and Fitness ===

Lockdown

In this book, it is assumed that the gyms are open so exercises with some typical gym machines are proposed.

In periods of lockdown, we can replace most of the exercises with some equipment that we can use, or already have, at home: a basic set includes a bench, one or more sets of dumbbells, a pull-up bar.

All items can be easily purchased new or used. The most important thing is to have enough loads to stimulate muscle growth.

It is possible to replace the lack of adequate weight with an increase in the number of repetitions. This guarantees improvements especially for those not looking for increase strength.

To increase strength, weights must push the muscle to adapt its capacity and structure to the weight lifted, so it's important to have more loads.

The rule: little movement is better than no movement.

More complex is the work to be done outside the gym related to the legs in which we have to replace the machines such as presses, leg extensions, and leg curls with squats and lunges, increasing the number of repetitions and using the dumbbells here too.

If we really can't get any tools we can perform free body exercises such as push-ups, crunches, squats, lunges, and all their infinite variations that allow us at least to keep fit.

In this case, I advise you to adopt a plan that involves performing 50 push-ups per day, 50 bodyweight squats, and 50 crunches and increase the number up to 100 repetitions, divided into sets of 20, 25. With half an hour a day, you will feel like a tiger!

If you are not trained enough, set yourself the goal of reaching that level after one or two months, starting from where you are and increasing by 10 repetitions every day or every week, according to your starting form.

The secret lies in the willingness to perform one, two, three more repetitions every time you train: the muscles tone up making them work, they are made for that, and in the meantime increases the metabolism and energy consumption.

=== Woman and Fitness ===

MEASUREMENTS AND INDICES

Functional Evaluation

With functional evaluation, we can monitor the performance of a subject and then evaluate whether the program is progressing in the desired direction. As far as bodybuilding is concerned and to set the training schedules, some tests are important that allow you to know the **maximum** in a given exercise.

As we saw in another chapter, the training tables take into account the percentages of load compared to the maximum load in a given exercise. Furthermore, performing the tests at the end of each mesocycle can testify to the increase or decrease in strength of an athlete and therefore allows you to correct the variables of training or nutrition.

1RM Test

5 are performed by establishing which maximum weight it was possible to lift by the subject, increasing the weight with each lift.

Brzycki's formula

With this formula, the maximum of the subject can be obtained indirectly through the number of repetitions performed with a given load.

1 theoretical RM = lifted load / [1.0278 - (0.0278 x repetitions performed)]

Heart rate

This parameter can be useful for monitoring the state of fatigue and also for setting various training programs. Starting from the approximate calculation of the maximum heart rate given by 220 - age, we can derive the optimal heart rate percentages based on the goal you have:

For cardiovascular training, 70-80% of the HR Max
For weight loss 60-70% of the HR Max
For moderate activity, 50-60% of the HR Max

For a more precise calculation, the Karvonen formula can be used, which takes into account the resting heart rate. In this way, the reserve heart rate is obtained, which is multiplied by the percentage of work you want to keep and added to the resting heart rate provides the heart rate to keep during physical activity, as per the following formulas.

Reserve HR (HRres) = HRmax - Resting HR
relative intensity = HRres X % HRris + Resting HR

Measurements and indices

Why take the measure.

In any area of human activity, the measurement of some parameters allows us to know the starting point and to define the goal to be achieved. In our case, when talking about body recomposition or changes in the body, some measurements help us to understand if our nutrition and training efforts are going in the right direction. Starting from elementary measurements such as weight, body temperature, heartbeat, or the circumferences of some areas of the body, we can later define some indices that give an idea of the general state of a subject and/or if we are indeed moving towards the established goal.

Bodyweight

It is one of the simplest measures to detect but it is subject to many variables. It is preferable to take it in the morning as soon as you get up, and make an average of the weekly data because weight changes are influenced by different factors: how much you ate the day before or how much fluids you lost. It cannot be established in advance whether the increase or decrease is due to the purchase or loss of lean or fat mass. However, it is easy to use.

Height

It is self-explanatory, useful for building some other indexes.

Temperature

Taken 10 minutes after getting up, measured 3 or 4 times, and then averaged. It is especially useful in a phase of caloric restriction to check if the metabolism is active or starts to stall. If we notice a decrease in temperature and the weight does not drop, it means that we must resort to a break in the diet until the temperature starts to rise again.

Heartbeat

Measured every morning, before getting out of bed and also after 15 minutes, then averaging the two data.

This data allows us to understand if the body is approaching a phase of temporary fatigue (overreaching) and allows us to understand when to insert a week of discharge, with lighter workouts. When the heartbeat increases compared to the initial readings by 15-20 beats, it is the signal that is the moment for discharge.

Circumferences: waist, abdomen, hips, thigh

To be detected in the morning as soon as you wake up every 7 or 14 days. Every 7 days if you are following a weight loss plan, 14 in a bulking phase, because changes in the waistline are quicker to see in a slimming phase, while the purchase of lean mass is slower.

These are the measurements I recommend:

Rib cage

Left and right arm flexed

Left and right leg

Forearm

Waist

The line above the belly button about 2 cm.

The line at the belly button level

The line below the belly button about 2 cm.

The three measurements at the abdominal level allow you to check whether the weight loss plan is correct because in many cases the weight loss proceeds from the upper abdomen towards the lower one. While if we are running into a phase of catabolism this is evident first in the limbs, hence the need to monitor the forearms and calves as well. For example, if the limbs but not the abdomen decrease the measurements while the scale goes down, it can mean that the body draws energy from the lean mass at the expense of the fat one in a period of caloric restriction.

7 site skin-fold plicometry

With the skin folder, we have an approximate measurement of subcutaneous fat and can be used to monitor the progress of efforts towards weight loss. These are the usual skin-site:

Abdomen

Iliac

Flank

Triceps

Subscapularis

Leg

They can be used to derive indices even if their detection is sub
ject to the imprecision of the taken by the detector. For this, it is
usually recommended to use an average of three measurements
for each point.

Fasting blood sugar

This parameter, to be measured in the morning on an empty
stomach, allows us to understand if the body triggers a form of
insulin resistance, that is if the nutrients are no longer captured in
the muscles. This measure can be especially useful in a bulking
phase to understand when it is time to stop the high-calorie diet
and decrease calories to improve cellular receptivity and limit the
number of nutrients that end up in fat cells. Values should be between 60 and 100 mg/dl.

INDICES

With some of the measures acquired, through mathematical formulas, some indices can be obtained that allow you to understand the fitness level and consequently monitor the progress of the path taken.

TDEE

TDEE is the acronym for Total Daily Energy Expenditure. It is the total number of calories burned on a given day and is the sum of four key factors:
basal metabolic rate
 thermic effect of food
 non-exercise activity thermogenesis
 exercise activity thermogenesis

Basal metabolic rate (BMR)

Basal metabolic rate refers to the number of calories burned by the body each day to allow the body to survive. BMR is the number of calories the body should consume in 24 hours at full rest.

Thermal effect of food (TEF)

When we eat food, our body has to spend energy to digest the food we eat which corresponds to about 10% of the energy introduced but it depends on the type of food ingested.

Non-exercise activity thermogenesis (NEAT)

Non-training activity thermogenesis (NEAT) constitutes the number of calories consumed during daily movement that is not classified as training. NEAT is highly variable from person to person and can play a rather large or small role in your overall TDEE depending on how physically active your work or daily events are.

Thermal effect of training (TEA)

The thermal effect of training is the number of calories burned as a result of physical exercise. Similar to NEAT, the thermal effect of training depends a lot on the effort made in a given training session so it is a parameter influenced by many variables.

The TDEE is the sum of these four values, so to put the parameters in a mathematical equation, for simplicity, here is the formula for calculating the TDEE:

TDEE = BMR + TEF + NEAT + TEA

When all these numbers are added together, you get an estimate of the number of calories needed daily to maintain your current weight for the same physical activity. Researchers have developed a set of models for calculating BMR, and one of the most used and simplest to calculate is the Harris-Benedict equation, which takes into account age, height, and weight.

BMR women = 655 + (9.6 x weight in kg) + (1.8 x height in cm) - (4.7 x age in years)

Male BMR = 66 + (13.7 x weight in kg) + (5 x height in cm) - (6.8 x age in years)

For example, if we take a 40-year-old male who is 175 cm tall and weighs 80 kilos we will have:

BMR = 66 + (13.7 x 80) + (5 x 175) - (6.8 x 40)

BMR = 66 + 1096+ 875 - 272

BMR = 1765 kcal.

Based on these values, the subject needs to consume about 1765 calories to stay alive without moving. The other components of the TDEE calculation can be estimated through a set of parameters that have been identified by scholars over time, the most used is a set of "activity multipliers", called Katch-McArdle multipliers. To calculate the approximate TDEE, simply multiply these activity factors by the BMR, defined based on the amount of movement performed by the subject on average:

Sedentary (little or no exercise + desk work) = 1.2

Slightly active (light exercise 1-3 days a week) = 1.375

Moderately active (moderate exercise 3-5 days a week) = 1.55

Very active (heavy training 6-7 days a week) = 1.725

Extremely active (very heavy exercise, hard work, training 2 times a day) = 1.9

So if for example, the subject is "Slightly Active" to calculate the approximate TDEE just multiply the BMR by 1.375. This gives us:

=== Woman and Fitness ===

TDEE = 1.375 x BMR
TDEE = 1.375 x 1765
TDEE = 2.427 kcal.

In this case, to maintain the current weight, the subject must introduce about 2,400 kcal per day.

Knowing the TDEE allows us to have a starting point from which to plan the path to follow to achieve the set goals and to be able to set up a food plan in a more precise way.

If you want to lose fat, we now know that we need to introduce less kcal than the current TDEE.

Knowing that 1 kg of fat corresponds to about 7,000 kcal, we should reduce the calorie intake by about 1,000 kcal per day to lose one kg of fat in a week. But during the slimming process not only fat mass is lost but also liquids and lean mass, for this reason, other measures must also be taken and studied, such as the measurement of circumferences or skin folds.

LBW (Lean Body Weight) lean body weight, is used for obtaining the percentage of body fat. The weight and measurement in centimeters of the abdominal circumference are used for this purpose.

With this index we can have an estimate of the amount of body fat, subtracting the lean mass from the total weight and then calculating a simple proportion. It is useful for monitoring the progress of the weight loss process.

Several formulas have been proposed for this index, here I show that of Wilmore and Behnke

LBW = 44.636 + 1.0817 (wt) - 0.7396 (c)

where wt stands for Body weight (in Kg.) and c stands for Abdomen circumference in centimeters.

Once the weight of the lean mass has been obtained, simply subtract it from the total weight to have an estimate of the fat mass and from this obtain its percentage relative to the total weight, that is

BF = Weight - LBW all measures in kg. where BF the fat mass in kg. Hence the fat percentage corresponds to 100 * BF / Weight

Ideal weight

The result of these mathematical formulas represents the ideal theoretical weight of the subject according to the author who proposed it. Below we present just a few.

Lorenz formula

This formula for calculating the ideal weight takes neither age nor skeletal structure into account, but it is widely used. Furthermore, it is not suitable for long-limbed and brachytype subjects.

Ideal weight Men = height in cm - 100 - (height in cm - 150) / 4

Ideal weight Women = height in cm - 100 - (height in cm - 150) / 2

Broca's formula

This formula for calculating the ideal weight is the simplest but takes into account only the height; the greatest limits lie in the non-correspondence of the ideal weight for medium-high stature.

=== Woman and Fitness ===

Ideal weight for males = height in cm - 100
Ideal weight for females = height in cm – 104

Wan der Vael formula
This formula considers height only:
Ideal weight Men = (height in cm - 150) x 0.75 + 50
Ideal weight Women = (height in cm - 150) x 0,6 + 50

Berthean formula
Ideal weight = 0.8 x (height in cm - 100) + age / 2

Perrault's formula
This formula takes into account age and height
Ideal weight = Height in cm - 100 + age / 10 x 0.9

BMI Body mass index
It is a generic indicator to define the physical state of a person concerning an ideal average based on the age, weight, height, and sex of the subject. This is the calculation: BMI = weight in kg / (height in meters * height in meters)

Below are the tables with the reference values for men and women.

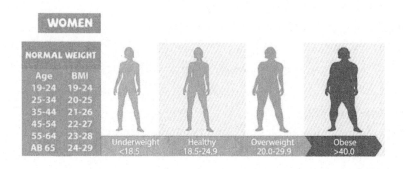

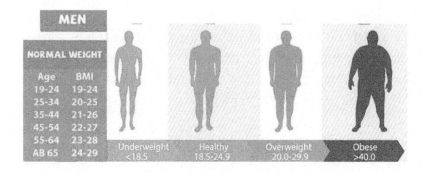

=== Woman and Fitness ===

Waist to Hip ratio

It is the ratio between waist circumference and hip circumference: Whr = Waist circumference / Hip circumference.

With this index, it is possible to determine the distribution of fat and therefore the biotype.

Below is a table that summarizes the data from the Waist / Hips ratio based on gender.

MEN		
	GYNOID	<=0.94
	NORMAL	0.95 – 0.99
	ANDROID	>1

WOMEN		
	GYNOID	<=0.78
	NORMAL	0.79 – 0.84
	ANDROID	> 0.85

Motivation

To model the body it takes time, it takes dedication, it takes patience.

You have to find the strength within yourself to train even when everything tells you to let it go.

After all, we all have dozens of distractions.

Many things tell us to choose the most comfortable way and the body itself tends to inaction.

To choose the most comfortable way.

We need **motivation and a positive mental approach**. In fact, as in all other aspects of life, the role of the mind is fundamental to achieving any result.

You must have **the will** not to give up your training routine. And the will must also be trained through a positive mental focus. But what does it mean?

It means going beyond the difficulties of the moment and looking at the final goal, at building muscle mass, at the physique you want to have, and always believing that it is achievable.

For this, it is necessary to set goals and plan the path to achieve them.

=== Woman and Fitness ===

Set goals

Having a goal is like seeing a lighthouse during an offshore storm. It allows you to stay on course towards what you want to be or become. This is why it is important to establish what you want to achieve: more muscles? less fat?

It is also important to give yourself a **reasonable time** to get it: I can't think of putting on 20 kg of muscle in a year of training, I can't think of losing 20 kg in a month without some decompensation. And it is better to set the goal precisely: I want to lose 10 kg in six months, I want to have 5 kg more muscle in a year. In this way, it will be easier to measure whether the direction taken is the correct one, the one that leads to the achievement of the goal. It will be easier to measure progress or stalls and take action accordingly.

Once the goal has been established, this must always be remembered at every training session, whenever you don't want to train, and even when you don't seem to get the desired results.

You must never stray from your goal. In defining the goal, it is necessary to go into details, break down the goal into **many smaller, more easily achievable phases**, create monthly, weekly, daily routines.

This way you can set measurable goals for each period, for example losing 0.5 kg per week means 12 kg in 6 months and focus on achieving this weekly goal.

You must always remember that in body recomposition the time factor counts, you must give your body time to adapt to the new situation and give it time to break homeostasis. You must want to achieve the goal, so ask yourself what you want to achieve. And everything will become easier.

Then take action, prepare a training plan, and follow it consistently. The confidence gained in seeing constant small improvements will give you the strength and energy to continue towards the goal.

Maximum concentration

When training, you should focus on the movement you are doing, feel which muscle is contracting, check if the posture is correct, in short, you must try to be focused on yourself.

Continuous experimentation

You have created your plan or used one of those provided in the book and you follow it faithfully, with constancy and discipline, but may it happen that in a training session you feel more tired or bored from the usual routine?

It is time to try something new, try an exercise that you haven't done for a long time or that you have never done, change the load, increase or decrease the repetitions. This way can help you resume your usual pattern in the following days with greater vigor. Because it is important to complete the training schedule for the set period without constantly changing exercises: you need to build willpower to stay fixed on the established course.

Push hard

We can combine it with concentration: the more concentrated you are, the more you can push hard: completing a work session that is training does not mean you must break the muscle fibers every time; it means giving your best for how you feel that day: if you feel tired because you slept little or ate badly, *give your best in those conditions*, but never give up, never give up on the planned training.

=== Andrea Raimondi ===

=== Woman and Fitness ===

BODY RECOMPOSITION

Body Recomposition

In practical terms, body recomposition has the purpose of reducing the percentage of fat mass and increasing the percentage of lean mass, that is, ultimately, of the muscles.

Hence the need to combine adequate nutrition with proper training.

As far as training is concerned, it is essential to ensure progression in the parameters that constitute it, parameters that we have described in the chapter dedicated to training variables.

However, the progression must depend on the phase of the protocol in which we find ourselves: if we are in a phase of reduction of fat mass, therefore in a period of calorie deficit, it is useless to try to set up a strength training, that is with high loads.

Instead, it is necessary to set up a workout that stimulates calorie consumption and is therefore set to increase metabolic efficiency, with lower loads, higher repetitions, and shorter recoveries between one series and another.

As for the food or rather an energy side, in the initial phase of the protocol, it is essential to calculate how many kilocalories are introduced. To this end, it is useful to keep a food diary on what and how much you eat for one or two weeks. Based on these data, **TDEE** is calculated.

The initial phase of all protocols requires that this caloric level is reached and stabilized for a certain period.

=== **Woman and Fitness** ===

To organize a meal plan, certain amounts of macronutrients are usually set to keep fixed, especially as regards the number of proteins and fats.

These quantities are related to the **lean mass** (eg: 3 g. Of protein per kg of lean mass; 0.8 grams of fat per kg of lean mass) and we act on the number of carbohydrates which are, we remember, the preferred energy source. of the human body.

The fundamental principle of body recomposition is given by the consideration that, by depriving or strongly reducing the intake of carbohydrates, the stocks of glucose present in the liver and muscles are reduced over time and these must be replaced as an energy source by catabolism of fat cells.

This process generates a series of biochemical reactions which, on the one hand, make the body more receptive to the supply of sugars during the so-called "refills" of carbohydrates, and on the other, allow you to use more fat reserves.

I am not going to dwell here on the fact that each of us has, by body constitution, a certain percentage of "physiological" fat given by his genetics and therefore it may be easier for a subject to move the adipose deposits than for another subject.

With constancy, commitment, and the right approach, anyone can bring their body (and mind) to change, beyond the starting point.

To scientifically set up a body recomposition procedure, it is essential to have as much data as possible available.

Some of this data is useful to be collected daily, such as temperature, heart rate, and weight, while others, such as circumferences, every week.

It is also essential to take note of what you eat during the day to estimate the weekly calorie intake, keeping a food diary as we said.

Based on these data, we can calculate some of the indices seen in the previous chapter that will serve us to better monitor the progress of the protocol.

It must always be borne in mind that changes in the body are not sudden but occur over more or less long periods: let's say that to see the effects of the work done, you have to wait from 20 to 30 days.

In practice, there is little point in fasting one day and then binging the next; what matters is the **weekly average** of calories introduced. Talking about calories as an end in themselves makes no sense. Counting calories makes sense if we can then relate them to a "threshold" level that allows us to establish whether it is necessary to increase or decrease the number of calories to be introduced, to obtain weight gain or loss.

For this reason, over time the calculation of the TDEE was introduced which defines the total amount of energy, in the form of calories, consumed by the body to maintain a given level of activity (i.e. energy consumption), including energy necessary to keep the organism alive, as already seen.

It is therefore clear that this "basic" or "minimum" energy level depends above all on how much energy is consumed on average during a day: those who perform hard work will have, under the same physical conditions (height, age, sex), a higher TDEE level. tall of those who work in front of a computer.

Furthermore, stress levels also influence these parameters.

For the moment, however, the reference component concerns the greater or lesser physical effort.

The starting point of all reasoning regarding a body recomposition is the assumption of resetting the body, bringing the average daily consumption to the level of the right TDEE.

Once this caloric level has been reached and stabilized, it is possible to start acting on the food variables.

We can decide on a calorie deficit if you want to lose weight, or for a calorie surplus if you want to increase lean mass.

In this second case, the challenge is not so much to increase the weight but to favor the muscular component over the fat component of the weight gain itself. And it is precisely here that science must merge with experience because the response of an organism to the modification of certain variables is not the same as the response of that of another organism. what little we can do.

But be careful not to overdo this idea.

If even genetically the composition of our muscles (in slow-twitch and fast-twitch fibers) is different from subject to subject and the percentage of genetic fat differs from individual to individual, this does not mean that **with the right commitment and an adequate path for this purpose, anyone who can improve their physical state**.

Surely this is possible, especially for those starting from scratch, from situations of overweight or little or no practice with training.

If this path is constantly monitored, through the detection of some measures at least weekly, it allows us to intervene promptly, modifying the variables we have available.

We can broadly divide a body recomposition based on its duration.

We will have a **short-term** recomposition (a few months) or a **long-term** one (one or more years).

The short-term recomposition can be suitable for those who are little or not trained at all and perhaps have to lose fat mass: in a few months, it can radically change appearance; while the long-term recomposition implies a greater commitment and a will that already has to be trained.

This does not mean that it can also be used by those who are now beginning their journey towards the construction of a new physicist.

Within these two protocols, it is possible to identify some fundamental phases.

The phases differ between the two protocols, above all for the duration for which the relative parameters must be extended.

In all cases, it is essential to always have the main measurements under control: temperature, weight, circumferences, caloric intake.

Just keep a diary of measurements, foods, and workouts.

=== Woman and Fitness ===

For both short-term and long-term recomposition, we start by measuring the daily consumption of kilocalories.

The TDEE is established.

The **average** between the two values is then determined to establish a starting kilocalorie value, from which to set the daily and weekly quantities of macronutrients.

Let's see the two procedures in more detail.

Short-term body recomposition

The duration of this procedure depends on the starting point, that is, on how many calories we have to take or lose to reach the metabolic reset indicated by reaching the TDEE.

That is, it depends on what is the value of the average calculated, as mentioned above, concerning the calories introduced in the period of the measurements present in the food diary.

The diet for the duration of the protocol provides for high consumption of proteins, up to 3g / kg of lean mass, and to keep fats between 0.5 and 0.8 / g per kg of lean mass.

The rest of the calories we need will be obtained from carbohydrates.

It is, therefore, necessary to **calculate the lean mass**.

For this we use the Wilmore and Behnke formula:

LBW = 44.636 + 1.0817 (wt) - 0.7396 (c)

where wt represents the body weight in kg and c represents the abdominal circumference in cm.

A subject weighing 70 kg and having a circumference of 78 cm will have a lean mass of about 63 kg.

This will be the initial parameter on which to calculate the quantities of proteins and fats to consume.

If the subject has a TDEE of 2,200 Kcal and current consumption of 1,900 Kcal, the value to be achieved with the diet for the metabolic reset phase will be 2,200Kcal + 1,900Kcal / 2 = 2,050 Kcal.

Keeping the hypothesis seen above of 3g / Kg of lean mass of daily protein we will have 3 * 63 (which are the Kg of lean mass) = 189 g proteins which correspond to about 756 Kcal (we know

=== Woman and Fitness ===

that a gram of protein is worth about 4Kcal). While for fats we will have, assuming we have 0.6 g / kg lean mass, rounded up, 38 g of fat, which is equivalent to 351 Kcal. To reach the required level of 2.050 Kcal we must consume 943 Kcal in carbohydrates which correspond to about 236 g.

These are the values to start from.

Once this value has been stabilized and consolidated, the calorie-cutting phase can be started, decreasing the intake of carbohydrates based on the decisive cut.

At this point, the weeks necessary to reach that value are decided. When you reach the established calories, the values are maintained for a few weeks, usually 2 or 3, before starting the actual body recomposition phase.

This consists of a calorie-cutting phase combined with a workout that leads to breaking the body's homeostasis and causes it to consume more fat. This is because, in essence, you are consuming fewer calories from carbohydrates.

It is essential to always keep protein consumption high.

It is now a question of deciding how to cut calories.

There are several ways: all of them aim to introduce a weekly calorie deficit.

During the week we can make several choices: we can decide on a drastic cut in calories for the first 3-4 days, decreasing the calories to -50 / -70% of what is indicated by the TDEE, and then exceeding the caloric level of the TDEE for a DAY and keep the calorie level at the TDEE for the remaining two days, see chart 1 with a TDEE of 1600.

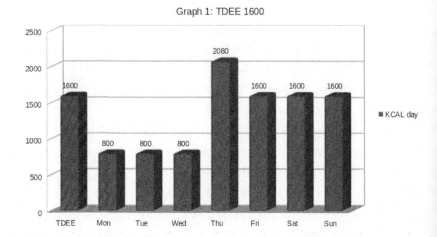

Graph 1: TDEE 1600

On calorie recovery days we lower protein consumption to 2g / kg of lean mass, keep fat at 0.5g / kg of lean mass and increase carbohydrates in order to reach or exceed the TDEE.

Or we can stay in a low-calorie diet (-50% TDEE) for the first three days and in a high-calorie diet (+10, + 20% calories compared to TDEE) for the next two days and then stabilize the intake with a normal calorie diet for the remaining days (i.e. with calories at the TDEE level), see graph 2.

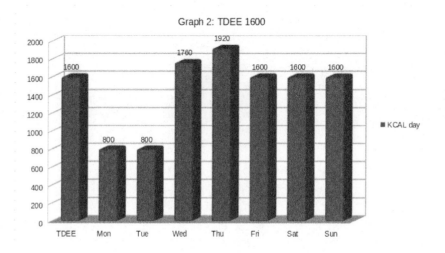

Or even stay low-calorie for the first three days (-40%, -50%, - 60% calories compared to the TDEE), in high calorie for the next two days (+20%, + 10% of calories compared to the TDEE) and then again in low calorie (-50% of calories compared to the TDEE) with the last DAY in a norm caloric diet at TDEE, illustrated by graph n.3. In all these cases, a caloric deficit is created.

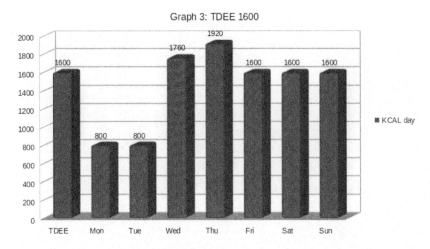

Training must focus on metabolic and cardiovascular work (or rest) in the low-calorie phase, and strength work, with few repetitions and high loads, in the high-calorie phases.
In the latter case, we can use those techniques typical of strength work, such as the pyramid series, supersets, 5x5s.

=== Woman and Fitness ===

While in metabolic work we reduce the rest between one series and another by increasing the number of repetitions with lower loads. This allows you to raise metabolic stress by adopting techniques such as tri-sets, giant sets, or circuit training, or even by increasing Aerobic Activity.

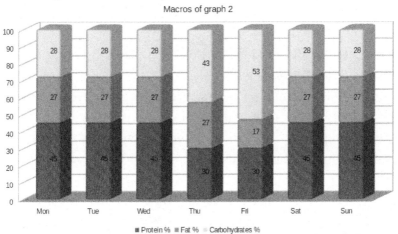

Graph showing the percentage breakdown of macronutrients related to the hypothesis of graph 2. In all the examples, the consumption of 3g / kg of lean mass for proteins and 0.8g / kg of lean mass for fats was held, the remaining amount to reach the caloric level required for carbohydrates. This is for low-calorie days. For the high-calorie days, Thursday and Friday, in this example, proteins dropped to 2g / kg lean mass and fats to 0.5g / kg lean mass: therefore the caloric share of carbohydrates increases to allow for an increase in insulin sensitivity. and start again with another week of calorie cutting.

Long-term body recomposition

In the long-term protocol, the low-calorie and high-calorie phases are used not (only) within the week but during the months.

In the phases of a long-term high-calorie diet, the goal will be to acquire muscles while limiting the increase in fat mass as much as possible. The increase in fat mass is a normal consequence of any high-calorie diet.

In the low-calorie diet phases, the key issue will be not to lose muscle mass while losing weight.

In the muscle-building phases, with a high-calorie diet, the workouts will be heavier than in the second case.

The starting point for the long-term protocol is to establish weekly weight gains, usually between 0.8 and 1% of kg of lean mass.

The average weekly gains can also be defined on the total weight, for women, we can indicate the gains between 0.4% of the total weight, with a maximum of 300 grams of increase, for beginners, and 200-250 grams of increase for athletes intermediate level, and 0.3%, with a maximum 100-150 grams increase, of the total weight, for the advanced level athletes.

However, keep in mind that if a person is already trained it is more difficult for him to increase with the indicated rhythms. For example, if we have a person who has 60kg of lean mass, the weekly increase must be:

between $60 * 0.8\% = 480$ and $60 * 1\% = 600g$ which corresponds to an increase in weekly Kcal ranging from 1.920 Kcal to 2.400Kcal, i.e. between 275 and 340 Kcal per day.

=== Woman and Fitness ===

To achieve these weekly increases, calories are increased but always respecting the previously reported parameters of proteins, fats, and carbohydrates.

How much to increase compared to the initial TDEE? Also in this case there is no single way. It depends on how the subject responds: you can start by increasing the calories by 10% or 20% compared to the TDEE and then adjust through the changes highlighted by the measures that are recorded.

Also in this phase, the need to detect what is happening is emphasized: if we realize that the weight increases excessively, we can intervene immediately by changing the calorie intake or increasing some training parameters.

Or again, body temperature will help us understand when the time has come to take a break from a low-calorie diet: if we start this period with a temperature of 36.5 degrees and after a few weeks this parameter starts to drop, it is an indication that the body begins to reduce its metabolic activity, because under stress: it may be the case to insert a break in the diet by inserting a so-called carbohydrate "refill" and modify the workouts until the temperature starts to rise again towards its initial value.

The same parameter of body **temperature** is used in the phases of construction or "mass" or, as we say in English for "bulk", to understand when we are reaching a point of momentary overtraining.

The weight and the measurement of the amount of lean mass, calculated through the circumferences as seen above, are useful for us to understand if we are going towards the goal of muscle gro-

[301]

wth as "clean" as possible, that is, without excessive increases in fat mass.

In this case, it is good to foresee phases (weeks) of caloric cutting, of "cut", within the mass period.

For example, we can decide, after 12-15 weeks of high calorie, to set 5-7 weeks of low calorie, trying to lose 1% of body weight per week.

So, for example, if we have an athlete who weighs 70kg after the weeks of mass we will have to lose 70 * 1% = 700g per week.

Which corresponds to the level of calories to have to consume 700 * 7 Kcal / g = 4,900 Kcal less per week. Which means 700 Kcal less per day.

The 7 Kcal / g used to calculate the Kcal to be removed represent the actual calories that are used by consuming one gram of body fat: 7,000 Kcal are contained in one kg of body fat.

However, we must always think keeping in mind the final result: overall, at the end of the weeks of calorie cutting, we will have to lose 4,900Kcal * 5 weeks (or for how many weeks it has been decided), which corresponds to a total loss of 24,500Kcal.

Now it is up to us to decide the strategy to be adopted to reach that level: we can decide on a constant cut of 4,900Kcal per week, or a decreasing calorie cut, starting with an initial clearer cut, for example of 6,500Kcal and so on. go down as the weeks go by 6,500 the first, 5,500 the second week and 5,000 calories the third week, 4,000 the fourth and 3,500 calories the fifth week.

=== Woman and Fitness ===

Nothing prevents us from following other paths, the important thing is to reach the overall cut of 24,500Kcal, considering the example above.

In the **period of a low-calorie diet** of long-term body recomposition, we will have days with calorie cuts but it is also useful to introduce high-calorie days.

Also in this case the optimal amounts of proteins and fats must always be kept fixed, increasing or decreasing carbohydrates.

You should not think about going down too quickly with calories, otherwise, muscle catabolism will increase.

Instead, let's assume a loss ranging from 0.5% to 1% of body weight per week: on a 70Kg person, the loss should be from 350g to 700g per week.

This corresponds to removing between 2,450 Kcal (350g * 7Kcal / gr. body fat) and 4,900 Kcal per week, i.e. between 350Kcal and 700Kcal per day.

Knowing, at this point, the weekly cut, we have to decide how to make this calorie cut within the week.

Cutting could take place constantly, or in a decreasing way or in a cyclical way, varying the intake of carbohydrates and fats but always leaving an optimal consumption of proteins.

In this phase, what has been said above regarding the cutting phase within the bulking period is valid, that is, to perform workouts that accompany the caloric cut and facilitate an increase in metabolic activity, through the reduction of recoveries between sets and increasing repetitions, using medium loads (65% -75% 1RM).

As already mentioned, only by keeping track of the path taken through regular measurements can we intervene in time and correct the route.

Only with time and consistency in training can we achieve the goals we have set ourselves. Whatever they are.

BIBLIOGRAPHY

Arienti, Giuseppe, Le basi molecolari della nutrizione, 3.Ed., Padova, Piccin, 2011

Delavier Frederic, The Strenght Training Anatony, Human Kinetic,(2011)

Esposito, Daniele, Project Diet 1 e 2, Milano, Project Invictus (2017)

Esquerdo, Óscar Maria Enciclopedia degli esercizi di muscolazione, Cesena, Elika srl Editrice (2011) Or.Ed. (2008)

Ferlito, Alessio Project Strenght, Brescia, Project Invictus (2016)

Johnston, Brian D., Eccellenza Tecnica, Firenze, Sandro Ciccarelli Editore, (2007), Or.Ed. (2003)

Johnston, Brian D., La scienza dell'esercizio, Firenze, Sandro Ciccarelli Editore, (2006), Or.Ed. (2003)

Lafay, Olivier Il Metodo Lafay , Milano, L'Ippocampo, (2011)Or.Ed., Parigi (2004)

Lehninger, Albert L., Principles of Biochemistry (1982)

Liparoti, Fabrizio Project bodybuilding, Brescia, Project Invictus (2018)

Lyle McDonald Ultimate Diet 2.0 (2004)

Lyle McDonald The Stubborn Fat Solution (2008)

McArdle, Katch, Katch Exercise Physiology (1994)

Neri M.,Bargossi A.,Paoli A Alimentazione fitness e salute, Cesena, Elika, (2002)

Roncari, Andrea Project Exercise vol 1 e 2, Milano, Project Invictus (2017-2018)

Schoenfeld, Brad Science and development of muscle hypertrophy (2016)

Schoenfeld, Brad The M.A.X. Muscle Plan (2013)

Schwarzenegger, Arnold, The new Encyclopedia of Modern Bodybuilding, New York (1998)

Wineck Jurgen, Optimales Training, 15.Ed. (2007)

Weider Joe, Ultimate Bodybuilding (1988)

=== Woman and Fitness ===

=== **Andrea Raimondi** ===

©2021 Andrea Raimondi
www.fitnessedintorni.it

AREdit.com
Contacts: info@aredit.com

All rights reserved. No part of this book may be reproduced by any mechanical, photographic, or electronic process, or in the form of a phonographic recording; nor may it be stored in a retrieval system, transmitted, or otherwise copied for public or private use—other than for "fair use" as brief quotations embodied in articles and reviews—without prior written permission of the publisher.

Printed in Great Britain
by Amazon